How to Break Bad News to People with Intellectual Disabilities

A Guide for Carers and Professionals

Irene Tuffrey-Wijne

Foreword by Professor Baroness Sheila Hollins

Jessica Kingsley *Publishers*
London and Philadelphia

First published in 2013
by Jessica Kingsley Publishers
116 Pentonville Road
London N1 9JB, UK
and
400 Market Street, Suite 400
Philadelphia, PA 19106, USA

www.jkp.com

Library of Congress Cataloging in Publication Data
Tuffrey-Wijne, Irene, 1963-
How to break bad news to people with intellectual
disabilities : a guide for careers and professionals /
Irene Tuffrey-Wijne ; foreword by professor Baroness Sheila Hollins.
p. cm.
Includes bibliographical references and index.
ISBN 978-1-84905-280-1 (pbk. : alk. paper) -- ISBN 978-
0-85700-583-0 (electronic text) 1. People with
mental disabilities. 2. Interpersonal communication.
3. Bad news. 4. Communication. I. Title.
HV3004.5.T84 2012
362.301'4--dc23
201201430

British Library Cataloguing in Publication Data
A CIP catalogue record for this book is available from the British Library

ISBN 978 1 84905 280 1
eISBN 978 0 85700 583 0

Printed and bound in Great Britain

'I found this book a pleasurable read, despite the delicate subject matter. It is clearly written and is full of examples that are instantly recognisable in my daily practice. The book highlights the importance of helping clients understand bad news situations regardless of their level of intellectual disability, and proves how including a client's support network in the process can be crucial in ensuring that bad news is successfully relayed. Practical and easily accessible, this book finally provides us with a set of solid guidelines to support our practice!'

– Marja Oud, palliative care lead and unit manager in a residential facility for people with intellectual disabilities, Netherlands

'As a parent, I wish I had been able to use this book by Dr Irene Tuffrey-Wijne when my daughter was slowly dying. Her guidelines are realistic, reassuring and rooted in a deep understanding of the highly individual needs of people with intellectual disabilities. It makes total sense to me that breaking bad news is a process, not an event. It demonstrates that it is possible to support someone with intellectual disabilities to come to terms with painful issues.'

– Jan Sunman, parent carer and participant in Dr Irene Tuffrey-Wijne's research

CONTENTS

LIST OF FIGURES

Foreword

Irene Tuffrey-Wijne has written a thoroughly researched and clinically sound primer on how to break important, life-changing news to people with intellectual disabilities, including those on the autistic spectrum. Irene sets the scene by reminding us of the extra communication challenges facing people with intellectual disabilities and all of us who care about and for them. She explains the limitations of existing 'bad news protocols' for this group of people, and I think rather subtly succeeds in showing that something that works better for people with intellectual disabilities will probably work better for most other people too!

She debunks common myths and assumptions, and deftly turns these into the foundation stones for her new guidelines. Her advice to identify the right-sized chunks of information for each person to build knowledge and increase decision-making capacity is deceptively simple. Of course building a good enough map of someone's information needs will require collaboration between family, staff and professionals, and in working together to do this the basis of a multidisciplinary care plan will be created too. She gives helpful worked examples of preparing people with different communication needs for different life-changing decisions.

All of us who provide support to people with these developmental cognitive disabilities will learn a great deal. This is a wise book deeply embedded in scholarly research and direct patient care, and I commend it to everyone concerned about someone with intellectual disability and their future. Moreover, I predict that Irene's ground-breaking guidelines will have a profound influence beyond Irene's own immediate current field of practice.

Professor Baroness Sheila Hollins
House of Lords, London

ACKNOWLEDGEMENTS

A book of this nature cannot be written by one person in isolation. The ideas presented here are the result of seven years of research and reflection. The research included the 'Veronica Project' (a study of the experiences of people with intellectual disabilities who had cancer, published by Jessica Kingsley Publishers in 2010) and then, more specifically, a two-year study that focused on 'how to break bad news'. Around two hundred people have taken part in my research over these seven years, including people with intellectual disabilities, families, friends, paid care staff, doctors and nurses in hospitals and hospices, and nurses and other professionals in intellectual disability services. They cannot be named individually, but they were crucial in helping me develop my understanding. Many of these participants shared deeply personal and often painful experiences, and I am grateful for their generosity and trust. I hope this book does them justice.

There are other un-named contributors. New knowledge emerges through listening to and discussing with others, and there have been numerous people who have inspired and guided me: friends; colleagues; people attending my teaching sessions, workshops and conference presentations.

I am very grateful to the Bupa Foundation for funding the research that underpins this book. They were extremely supportive throughout, accommodating my need to take time out when bad news situations overtook my personal life. Simultaneously, Macmillan Cancer Support funded a study of the experiences of people with intellectual disabilities who had a relative or friend with cancer; that study, too, contributed to the development of my guidelines for breaking bad news.

My research team at St George's, University of London, was invaluable. Niki Giatras gave support with the focus groups and managing the data. Gary Butler and Amanda Cresswell co-facilitated the focus groups with people with intellectual disabilities; these two colleagues, who have intellectual disabilities themselves, not only added crucial insights but also enabled participants with intellectual disabilities to contribute more fully. Sheila Hollins provided supervision: gentle, wise and always encouraging. Jane Bernal has helped me put my ideas into words for over a decade, often challenging and thought-provoking, always down to earth, relevant and with a lightness of touch. Her input on mental capacity has been particularly useful.

The 'breaking bad news' study was supported by a Research Advisory Board chaired by Sheila Hollins (professor in intellectual disability, St George's, University of London). This group met regularly, providing guidance and giving feedback on the findings. Thank you to Paul Adeline (researcher and advisor with intellectual disabilities, St George's, University of London); Peter Cranham (self-advocate, Acttoo Theatre Company); June Allen (lead cancer nurse), Patrick Stone (consultant in palliative medicine), Jim Blair (consultant nurse in intellectual disability), Valerie Emmons (cancer patient group, 'Improving the Cancer Experience'), Monica Stannard and Pauline Stanley (family carers, Caring Solutions), all at St George's Hospital, London; Jane Bernal (consultant psychiatrist, Cornwall Partnership NHS Trust); Leopold Curfs (professor in intellectual disability) and Ireen Proot (senior researcher), both at Governor Kremers Centre, Maastricht University, Netherlands; Susannah Seyman and Stuart Mills (Down Syndrome Association); Lucy Virgo (family liaison officer, Mencap); and Sue Martin (speech and language therapist, Islington Learning Disability Partnership).

A number of people read the first draft of the manuscript and gave very helpful feedback and suggestions about the content, structure and style. This book is much better as a result of their efforts. Many thanks therefore to June Allen, Jane Bernal, Pete Crane, Leopold Curfs, Jason Davidson, Valerie Emmons, Niki Giatras, Lesley Gibbs, Florika Grigoras, Sheila Hollins, Sue Marsden, Sue Martin, Pauline Stanley, Mike Stannard, Aaron Sutherland, Astrid Ubas, Lucy Virgo and Astrid Wijne.

My mother, Rosa Wijne, and my sisters, Ingrid and Astrid, have added depth and understanding as I was shaping my ideas about breaking bad news. Contending with my mother's life-threatening and life-changing diagnoses forced me to step out of my professional role and into the much more important and demanding role of family member. I tried not to let my job interfere with that role, but there is no denying that our own bad news journey has influenced my work and this book.

Finally, a few personal notes of thanks. To Florika, for sustaining me with music and friendship whilst working on this book. Most of all, thanks to Michael, Dominic, Clara and Susanna for sustaining me with life, love and laughter. They made me see again and again that life is very good news indeed – and they let me hog the top room to write in.

PART I

Background

CHAPTER I

Introduction

HOW NOT TO BREAK BAD NEWS

'Twenty-two years ago I was a very raw student nurse. There was David, who had intellectual disabilities and was living with his sister, and for seven years he'd been asking his sister every day where Dad was. His sister had explained that Dad was in hospital. Dad had actually died seven years earlier. And I was asked as a young student nurse to go along and break the bad news of his father's death. I was very poorly skilled. I can remember explaining to David that his dad had gone to heaven, to which he responded, "What? Dad is in the oven?!" It was very, very poorly handled…

'I just wanted to break the news at the time, to get it over with quickly and somehow hope that the matter would be settled, that this man would be satisfied. It was sometime later that I realized I was not the "right" person to break the news. Even to this day, I wish I could wind back the clock and start the dialogue with David again, so that there would be a better outcome for him and for me.'

– *Intellectual disability nurse*

'SHE WANTED TO PROTECT ME'

Amanda Cresswell has had her share of challenges in life. She was born with brain damage, leading to mild cerebral palsy and intellectual disabilities. Her mother died of a brain tumour when Amanda was 14. Amanda herself was diagnosed with non-Hodgkin lymphoma at the age of 30 and she went through an aggressive programme of treatments. There have been numerous other hardships for her.

When Amanda was asked what the most difficult time in her life had been, she said without a moment's hesitation: 'That my mum didn't tell me that she was sick. I still regret it now. She never told me that she was dying... She wanted to protect me. She used to be in a bad mood all the time, she used to shout at me, it was horrible. And of course I didn't understand why!'

'I WOULD LIE FOR HIS OWN GOOD'

'If my son was terminally ill, I would be very positive with him. If he asked me, "What's going to happen to me?" I think I'd lie. I'd lie for his own good. I'd say, "We'll see how you are and maybe in a week's time you'll be feeling better." I can't see the point in telling the end situation.'

– Father of a man with moderate intellectual disabilities

WHY DON'T WE BREAK BAD NEWS?

Nobody likes to break bad news. We worry about how to do it, how someone will respond, and how we will cope with their response. It may seem the easiest option not to break the news, or to get someone else to do it – even if they are clearly not suitable for the task, like the unfortunate student nurse quoted above. Many people even try to pretend that the bad news event hasn't happened. The example is extreme, but protecting people with intellectual disabilities from bad news still happens today. There are many reasons for this.

- 'She couldn't possibly understand it.'
- 'It will upset him. What's the point of upsetting him?'
- 'We don't know how she will react. She is quite an emotional person.'
- 'I'm not the right person to tell him. It should come from someone closer to him.'
- 'I don't have the skills. I don't know how to break bad news.'
- 'Her family doesn't want her to be told. We can't go against their wishes.'
- 'I don't have all the right information myself, so how can I tell her?'
- 'If he knows that he is going to die, his health will get worse. He will just give up.'

None of us like to hear bad news either. Many of us find it difficult to cope with significant changes in our lives, particularly if we feel that things are changing for the worse. People with intellectual disabilities often have a lot of experience with loss and change, and some are very resilient and accepting. But many people with intellectual disabilities need significant support in order to cope with life's changes.

BAD NEWS DOESN'T GO AWAY

Not telling someone about bad news doesn't make the bad news disappear. Bad news is often to do with change that will affect someone's life, whether or not you explain it and help him to understand it.

'WE SHOULD HAVE TOLD HER'

Sylvia White was a young woman with Down's syndrome. She was very close to her brother Steven, with whom she lived in the family home. When Steven had an accident that left him in a coma for months, Sylvia's family didn't know how to help her. Coping with their own distress was hard enough for them; they had no support in coping with Sylvia's too. Sylvia couldn't understand why there was such an enormous change in her life. She became angry. Later, when Steven was home in a wheelchair, she would lash out at him and tip his wheelchair over.

Years afterwards, Sylvia's sister reflected: 'Sylvia already knew that Steven was not at home. She kept asking for him. Not involving her was not protecting her, as we then thought. She knew, but she couldn't verbalize it. We should have told her, given her pictures of Steven and the hospital, taken her to visit him. Her behaviour became "challenging", when in fact it was Steven's accident and the change in her life circumstances that was challenging, not her!'

It is clear that breaking (or not breaking) bad news not only affects the person concerned, but also the bearers (or non-bearers) of bad news. Badly managed bad news situations can haunt us for years. Should we have done things differently? And if so, how? How can we face up to such difficult situations, cope with them ourselves, and help people with intellectual disabilities to understand and cope with them too?

This book will not provide all the answers. Bad news is exactly that: it is bad news, and guidelines cannot make the breaking of bad news easy, because it never is. It can be very tempting to try and dress it up as 'good news', glossing over the badness and sadness of the situation.

You are going to have a lovely new support worker! Isn't that wonderful! You are so lucky!

Instead of:

I'm really sorry but I am leaving. I am starting a new job. I won't be coming to work here any more.

Of course it is important to explain that there are positives, that there will be someone else to take over the job – but that is not the most significant change for someone to deal with. The major change will be that he won't see his favourite support worker any more.

ABOUT THIS BOOK

This book will give you some guidance about how to support someone with intellectual disabilities in bad news situations. I hope that this will help you to feel less 'lost', help you think about what you can do and who can support you, make you see the situation in a new light, give you ideas about how to do things better, or maybe simply reassure you that you are already approaching bad news situations in the best possible way. My hope is that nobody should come to 'wish to wind back the clock and start again', like the student nurse who left his client thinking that Dad was in the oven.

There must be a word of warning about the danger of writing guidelines. The process of developing the breaking-bad-news guidelines described in this book involved talking to many people, including parents. As one concerned parent explained:

My ex-husband died about six years ago, and I felt under pressure by the manager of my daughter's residential home to tell her in a certain way. It was almost like he had a 'model' of how he thought people should be told, and I just think it's so individual. So I must admit, when you said about developing a model, I felt myself… [pulls face of dislike].

The problem with guidelines is that they can only be described in a linear way, like a recipe: 'Do this, or think about this, then this, then this.' Of course, life isn't like that: it is fluid, unpredictable and highly individual. You may think you need to handle one type of situation, only to find that the other person has a completely different agenda or way of experiencing the situation. You may have thought very carefully about how you are going to explain to someone that the day centre is going to close down, planning what you will say, how you will say it and who you will involve – but when it comes to it, she shows no interest at all in your information, because she is preoccupied with what there is going to be for lunch; and you may find that there is never a time when she seems to be taking in what you want to explain.

This book is not meant to *dictate* how you break bad news, but rather to *guide and support* the process of helping someone with intellectual disabilities understand bad news. Your individual judgement must always take precedence.

Terminology
There is always the problem of using gender-neutral language. I have opted for using either 'he' or 'she' rather randomly, instead of the cumbersome 'he or she'.

I use the term 'intellectual disabilities', as currently this seems to be acceptable world-wide and is now increasingly used in international publications. Terminology changes all the time. In the not so distant past, the terms 'mental handicap' and 'mental retardation' were used widely, but these are now considered derogatory. The term 'learning disabilities' is widely used in the UK, but this can be confusing outside its borders, where 'learning disabilities' may be understood to mean specific learning difficulties such as dyslexia. Where I have used quotes, I have changed the speaker's use of 'learning disability' to 'intellectual disability' for the sake of consistency.

Who is this book for?
This book is relevant to a wide range of bad news situations, including, for example:
- 'Dad is going to die.'
- 'The dog has died.'
- 'You have cancer.'
- 'Your support worker is leaving.'
- 'The trip is cancelled.'
- 'We are going to move house.'
- 'The day centre is going to close down.'
- 'You have to go into hospital.'
- 'Mum and Dad are getting divorced.'

It will be useful for anyone who finds themselves in a bad news situation involving someone with intellectual disabilities. This can include:

- family carers
- other unpaid carers
- friends
- paid carers
- service managers
- health and social care professionals (doctors, nurses, social workers, allied health professionals) in a wide range of settings, such as:
  - intellectual disability services
  - primary and secondary health care services
  - hospices.

Some readers may be more familiar with certain concepts than others. Doctors, nurses and social workers may be very familiar with existing models for breaking bad news and may have received advanced communication skills training. Family carers and staff working in intellectual disability services may be very familiar with the way people with intellectual disabilities absorb and process information. In writing this book, I have tried not to assume any background knowledge and to keep it accessible for a wide readership.

The research underpinning this book

The guidelines described here are the result of a two-year study focusing exclusively on the issue of breaking bad news to people with intellectual disabilities. It involved focus group meetings and interviews with over 100 people across the UK, including people with intellectual disabilities, family carers, intellectual disability professionals and health care professionals (mostly doctors and nurses). This was combined with what we learned in previous studies, the literature, and my own professional and personal experience. More detailed information on how the study was conducted can be found in the academic literature (see Further Reading at the end of the book).

The guidelines for breaking bad news can also be found on the following website: **www.breakingbadnews.org**.

The examples in this book

Most of the examples in this book come from the study described above. Many quotes are verbatim, originating in tape-recorded interviews and focus groups. Some examples have come from other people I have met in the course of my work, such as those participating in workshops and training sessions. I have also used examples from my own professional experience. In most cases, I have changed the details very liberally in order to protect people's identities. All names are changed with the exception of Amanda Cresswell (at the start of this chapter), who has published and spoken publicly about her experiences and does not wish to be anonymous. A few examples, including all the examples in Part 4, are fictional but firmly based on real-life stories.

How this book is structured

- **Part 1** gives some background information about intellectual disabilities, breaking bad news, mental capacity, existing breaking bad news guidelines, and the need for new guidelines for people with intellectual disabilities.
- **Part 2** describes the new guidelines and underlying principles for breaking bad news to people with intellectual disabilities.
- **Part 3** explains the different aspects of the guidelines in more detail and suggests how they can be used in practice.
- **Part 4** gives three wide-ranging examples of how the guidelines can be applied in real-life situations. It highlights, in particular, how the way in which someone is helped to understand bad news has to be adapted to their very personal circumstances, abilities and needs.
- **Part 5 (The Appendices)** includes an at-a-glance overview of the guidelines and some guiding questions, as well as some useful resources.

The 'Thinking points' at the end of most chapters are designed to familiarize you more thoroughly with the content of the chapter, and to help you put that content into the context of your own experiences.

THINKING POINTS

- Have you ever had to break bad news to someone with intellectual disabilities? How well do you think the situation was handled?

- What did you find most difficult about it?

- Have you ever been in a situation where bad news was not disclosed, or not fully disclosed, to someone with intellectual disabilities? If so:

  ◦ Do you know why it was not disclosed?

  ◦ Who decided not to disclose the (full) truth?

  ◦ Was this decision made explicit? Were the reasons discussed?

CHAPTER 2

Intellectual Disabilities

DEFINITION

There are three aspects to intellectual disability:

a. Impaired intelligence.

b. A reduced ability to cope independently.

c. Starting in childhood, with a lasting effect on development.

All of these three aspects must be present if someone is to be described as having intellectual disabilities. People with Asperger's syndrome do not have intellectual disabilities because they have average or above-average intelligence. People with dementia, or people who sustained brain injuries in adulthood, do not have intellectual disabilities because their cognitive limitations did not start in childhood.

The new guidelines for breaking bad news have been developed specifically for people with intellectual disabilities, although many of the underlying principles will resonate with other groups – including the general population.

a. Impaired intelligence

Intelligence is a general mental ability which includes:

- reasoning
- planning
- solving problems
- thinking abstractly
- thinking logically
- comprehending complex ideas
- learning quickly
- learning from experience.

People with impaired intelligence find it much more difficult to understand new or complex information, or to learn new skills. It is not difficult to see how this aspect of intellectual disabilities affects the processing of bad news, which may include abstract concepts and can be highly complex in nature.

b. A reduced ability to cope independently

People with intellectual disabilities have significant limitations in their conceptual, social and practical skills. In practice, this can mean the following:

- **Conceptual skills:** language, the ability to read and write, and understanding concepts of money, time and numbers.
- **Social skills:** interpersonal skills, understanding social rules, social responsibility, self-esteem, gullibility, naivety (lacking judgement), following rules and obeying laws, actively avoiding being victimized, and social problem solving.
- **Practical skills:** activities of daily living, occupational skills, use of money, safety, health care, coping with independent travel and transportation, managing schedules and routines, and use of the telephone and computer.

c. Starting in childhood, with a lasting effect on development

In order to fall within the definition of 'intellectual disabilities', the difficulties described above must originate before the age of 18 and be life-long.

SOME IMPORTANT CONSIDERATIONS

- Intellectual disability should be seen within the context of someone's social environment and culture, taking into consideration what is typical for that person's peers.
- Depending on the available support, it is possible for someone with intellectual disabilities to improve their ability to cope and function over time. This includes coping with bad news situations.
- It is crucial that people are not just seen in terms of their weaknesses, but also in terms of their strengths. These

strengths can be considerable and may be a direct result of having intellectual disabilities. In my previous work, for example, I was struck by people's remarkable resilience as they were living and dying with cancer; this could be a result of having coped with a life of adversity, or an inherent ability to live in the present moment.

DEGREE OF INTELLECTUAL DISABILITY

The extent of limitations can vary hugely, but most people with intellectual disabilities will need some support in managing their daily lives, ranging from minimal (coping well with life unless something out of the ordinary happens) to around-the-clock support. There is also a huge variation in people's communication skills. At one end of the spectrum, someone may have excellent receptive and expressive verbal skills and may be able to grasp abstract concepts, including a concept of time and future; at the other end, someone may not be able to use or understand words at all and have little concept of things that are outside their immediate experience.

A distinction is often made between mild, moderate, severe and profound intellectual disabilities. It can be difficult to categorize people, but it may be helpful to describe some of the differences between people with mild to moderate intellectual disabilities and severe to profound intellectual disabilities. There are differences in communication and support needs which have an impact on the approach to breaking bad news.

- People with **mild and moderate intellectual disabilities:** likely to result in learning difficulties in school and possible developmental delays in childhood; most can learn to develop some degree of independence, and will be able to live and work in the community with varying levels of support; many will be able to maintain good social relationships. Most will acquire adequate communication skills.
- People with **severe and profound intellectual disabilities:** likely to result in continuous need for support, and possible severe limitations in self-care, continence and mobility. Communication skills will be severely limited.

Although the principles for breaking bad news are the same for everyone, the methods we need to use to help someone understand bad news must clearly be adapted to their intellectual capacity, social ability, communication ability and support needs.

Autism

Some people with intellectual disabilities also have autism. People on the autistic spectrum often have difficulty in recognizing other people's feelings and emotions and expressing their own. They find it particularly hard to predict what will happen next, to prepare for change and plan for the future, and to cope in new or unfamiliar situations. People with autism often like to have a strict daily routine in order to make sense of the world. Any changes in this routine can be very difficult and need much preparation and support.

I have highlighted the presence of autism in some of the examples in this book, because their specific characteristics mean that people on the autistic spectrum face particular challenges when coping with bad news and change.

HOW MANY PEOPLE HAVE INTELLECTUAL DISABILITIES?

An estimated 1–3 per cent of the world population have intellectual disabilities. The number of people with intellectual disabilities is rising, partly due to better survival rates in childhood and reduced mortality among older adults with intellectual disabilities.

There are no reliable statistics in the UK on how many patients admitted to hospital or other health care settings have intellectual disabilities. However, it is likely to be a sizable minority – if 2 per cent of patients have intellectual disabilities, this would be one in every 50 patients. A much larger proportion of patients will have someone in their close social circle with intellectual disabilities: a son or daughter, a sibling, a parent, an aunt or uncle. Breaking bad news about ill-health to people with intellectual disabilities (their own, or that of a relative) is not a marginal issue. If professionals have not encountered such a situation before, they either haven't been in their job for more than a couple of months, or they haven't realized that their patient/client/relative had intellectual disabilities, or their service is failing to provide equal access to people with intellectual disabilities.

THINKING POINTS

If your job involves working with the general population:

- How often do you encounter a patient/client/relative with intellectual disabilities?
- How easy or difficult is it for you to determine whether someone has intellectual disabilities?
- Are you familiar with your local intellectual disability services? If not, how can you find out more about them?

If your job involved working with people with intellectual disabilities, or if you are a relative or carer:

- How well do general health care professionals recognize, understand and support the needs of your patient/client/relative?

CHAPTER 3

What Is Bad News?

'YOU ARE BETTER – YOU NEED NO FURTHER TREATMENTS'

Valerie Goldsmith, who had moderate intellectual disabilities, was diagnosed with breast cancer. It was caught early and successfully treated. Valerie managed to go through all her investigations, coped well with the mastectomy and attended all follow-up appointments without difficulties, which surprised her carers, who described her as being 'quite challenging at times'. Her hospital consultant and his team considered whether Valerie needed any additional treatments, such as radiotherapy, but in the end they decided that this was not necessary. Together with the intellectual disability nurse, they gave Valerie the good news that they thought her cancer was cured and that she needed no further treatments.

Everyone was taken aback when Valerie started shouting and lashing out, both in the oncology department and on her return home. During the following days, it transpired that she viewed the information as 'bad news'. She believed that stopping the treatment would mean that she would not get as much individual attention, or have as many visits to the hospital, which she told her nurse she enjoyed 'even though I had cancer'.

IS IT NEWS, AND IS IT BAD?

When we talk about 'breaking bad news', we are making two assumptions, both of which may be wrong:

1. It is news. (Maybe she knew this already?)
2. It is bad. (Maybe she doesn't experience it as 'bad'?)

The opposite, of course, can also be true. We may talk about something and think someone knows it already, only to find that he doesn't (or he hasn't understood its full meaning) and is deeply shocked by it. We may think that our information is quite innocent or insignificant, or maybe even good news (as in the example above), but it is experienced as very bad news indeed.

Bad news is 'any news that drastically and negatively alters the patient's view of her or his future' (Buckman 1984, p.1597). In other words, it could be anything that makes your future look less bright than you had thought. This raises some immediate questions about someone's concept of future, and his ability for abstract thinking.

What does this person see as 'the future'?

Many people with intellectual disabilities, and particularly those on the autistic spectrum, have a very poor concept of time. This makes locating past and future events in time very difficult for them. The concepts of 'yesterday' or 'tomorrow' may not mean much. If someone cannot anticipate the future beyond this afternoon, then the news that Mum has to go into hospital next week may be experienced in two different ways: (1) it is not related to his immediate experience, and therefore is not experienced as 'bad news'; (2) it is experienced as 'bad news' for the whole week, because he cannot grasp that there is a time gap between 'now' and 'Mum going into hospital'.

What is someone's ability for abstract thinking?

If someone doesn't easily conceptualize things but experiences life mostly through what can be seen, heard and felt, then the news that a friend has dementia and will gradually lose their skills may not be experienced as bad news.

'BAD' IS SUBJECTIVE

BAD NEWS IS NOT HAVING ANY PUDDING

'My daughter never shows frustrations or upset if she doesn't see someone for weeks and weeks. So in a way, what is bad news to her? I'm not sure she even has that concept.'

'Bad news is if you said to my son he couldn't go to the disco on Monday night. That's *really* bad news!'

'For my daughter, bad news is: you can't have any pudding. Or we've run out of chocolate mousse!'

– Parents of people with severe and profound intellectual disabilities

Some of the examples I have used to explain and illustrate the guidelines for breaking bad news can seem trivial. Stories of moving house or a cancelled disco may not appear to be as important as stories of death and loss. However, a break with routine can be very upsetting for the person concerned; for some people, a cancelled disco is more real and can feel more devastating than the news that Dad has had a stroke.

NOT WORRIED ABOUT CANCER

Ben Edwards had severe intellectual disabilities and lived in a residential care home. He had advanced prostate cancer and his prognosis was poor. Ben was always present in the consulting room when the doctor discussed the cancer. His home manager said: 'It goes over his head, really. He doesn't really understand it. I try to explain things to him afterwards, but I keep it really simple. I think that's enough.'

Ben did not seem worried about his cancer and declining health, but he was worried about the immediate changes if his hospital appointments were late. The home manager explained: 'He is not like all the other people in the waiting room who are sitting there worrying about what the doctor is going to say, and what is going to happen to them. He is just worrying that it is taking too long and he can't get to his videos and his lunch on time.'

– Based on Living with Learning Disabilities,
Dying with Cancer *(Tuffrey-Wijne 2010, p.85)*

THINKING POINTS

Think about a real-life situation where A had to break bad news to B.

- To what extent was it 'news' to B? Did it come completely out of the blue, or did he already suspect or know it?

- Can you think of any examples where A broke 'bad news' to B, but B did not seem to experience it as particularly 'bad'?

- Can you think of any examples where what A thought was fairly innocent news was actually experienced as bad news by B?

CHAPTER 4

Breaking Bad News

Knowledge, Skills and Guidelines So Far

SHOULD BAD NEWS BE BROKEN?

Should doctors tell their patients that they have cancer? There are cultural differences: in some parts of the world, doctors do not tell patients routinely about a poor prognosis. However, in many parts of the Western world, the question itself seems rather out-of-date. Nowadays, an overwhelming majority of cancer patients and their relatives want their doctors to be open and honest, and to provide them with information. Health professionals agree: they believe mostly that realistic and truthful disclosure is preferred to withholding information, and most doctors and nurses prefer their patients to know that they are dying. This is a huge shift in attitude. A study in 1961 found that the vast majority of doctors did not tell cancer patients their diagnosis (Oken 1961).

There are three basic ideas about whether or not bad news should be broken: 'no, never' (non-disclosure); 'yes, always' (full disclosure, giving full information to the patient as soon as it is known); and 'yes, but it depends on the person' (individual disclosure). Each of these stems from a number of assumptions (Girgis and Sanson-Fisher 1995).

Non-disclosure:

- The doctor knows what is best for the patient, without reference to him.
- Patients do not want to know bad news.
- Patients need to be protected from bad news.

Full disclosure:
- The patient has a right to full information.
- All patients want to know bad news about themselves.
- It is appropriate for patients to make their own decisions, since they have to live with the consequences.

Individual disclosure:
- People differ in the amount of information they want.
- People differ in their ways of coping.
- Time is needed to absorb and adjust to bad news.
- A partnership between the doctor and the patient is in the patient's best interest.

What assumptions do we make?

If you ever had to decide whether or not to break bad news to someone with intellectual disabilities, it is worth reflecting on what influenced your decision about how much of the truth to disclose. Underlying thoughts could be, for example:
- Her family and carers know what is best for her. They will tell me whether or not to disclose the truth.
- People have a right to know, and that includes people with intellectual disabilities. We should tell her the full truth even if the family disagrees.

Decisions about what is best for someone are not always based on an individual assessment of her individual needs, preferences and coping styles: sometimes, they are based on an *assumption* of what is best for her.

Individually tailored disclosure

It is now generally accepted among medical and social care professionals that individually tailored disclosure is the preferred option. Although most patients will want to know their diagnosis, prognosis and treatment options, some people do not want full information about this. By telling people more than they want to hear, we may be preventing them from using 'denial' as an important psychological coping mechanism or defence. The question, therefore, is no longer 'Should bad news be broken?' but 'How should it be broken? And how much at a time?'

There have been huge advances in knowledge, skills and the provision of communication training for health care professionals. Most of this is based on scenarios where health care professionals, and doctors in particular, have to impart the bad news of a life-limiting condition or poor prognosis.

EXISTING GUIDELINES FOR BREAKING BAD NEWS

During the past decades researchers and clinicians have developed a range of guidelines for communicating bad news. These have also been called 'models' for breaking bad news, but I will use the word 'guidelines' – when I talked to people with intellectual disabilities about a model for breaking bad news, they thought I was referring to something to do with fashion!

Perhaps the most well-known guidelines were developed by Buckman, who called it a 'Six Step Protocol for breaking bad news', described in his seminal book *How to Break Bad News: A Guide for Health Care Professionals* (Buckman 1992). There have been numerous other guidelines, but they mostly follow the same linear, step-by-step approach. The existing guidelines recommend moving from 'preparing for disclosure' to 'disclosure' to 'follow-up'.

Prepare:
- Get the right setting, involve/invite significant others, sit down, look calm and attentive, convey that you are listening, switch off the phone.
- Find out how much the patient knows.
- Find out how much the patient wants to know.

Disclose:
- Give the patient a 'warning shot' by letting them know that bad news is coming.
- Clarify understanding.
- Give information step-by-step, in small chunks.

Follow up:
- Respond to emotions.
- Answer questions.
- Make a plan for follow-up meetings and support.

Poor communication can have a negative impact on patients and their families. About 10 per cent of written complaints received by UK National Health Service hospitals are about poor communication and information giving (The NHS Information Centre 2011). Being able to communicate with sensitivity, and to break bad news well, is therefore a key skill for clinicians. Existing guidelines for breaking bad news have made a huge and positive difference to the experience of patients and families.

USING THE EXISTING GUIDELINES FOR PEOPLE WITH INTELLECTUAL DISABILITIES

When the bad news situation involves someone with intellectual disabilities, there are clearly additional issues that need to be considered. A number of authors have tried to adapt the step-by-step guidelines to the needs of people with intellectual disabilities. These adaptations include:
- Take extra time.
- Involve the person's family.
- Involve the person's paid carers.
- Use simple language and pictures.
- Limit the amount of information.
- Expect and allow for non-standard responses, including behavioural changes.

However, as we will see in the next chapters, simply using the step-by-step protocols for breaking bad news (maybe with some adaptations to meet people's additional needs) is not straightforward. I believe that we need a new set of guidelines.

THINKING POINTS

Look at the 'Prepare/Disclose/Follow up' guidelines. Think about applying these to one or more people with intellectual disabilities that you know.

- Can you foresee any problem areas?
- Would any of the steps be particularly difficult?

CHAPTER 5

Why We Need New Guidelines for Breaking Bad News

PETE'S STORY

In 2008, I completed a three-year study into the experiences of 13 people with intellectual disabilities who had cancer. For ten people, the prognosis was poor. Almost everyone in that study – families, care staff, doctors and nurses – struggled with the question of when and how people with intellectual disabilities should be told that they had cancer, and (if this was the case) that they were going to die. They had little help and guidance on the matter. One highly trained and experienced consultant in palliative care tried to follow the existing guidelines for breaking bad news to Pete Carpenter in the case described below. Here, these guidelines actually seemed to hinder rather than help.

TELLING PETE THAT HE HAS END-STAGE CANCER

Pete Carpenter was 66 years old and had severe intellectual disabilities. He lived in a staffed residential care home. His speech was limited to short sentences. His intellectual and verbal limitations were not always immediately obvious, because he was highly sociable and an excellent mimic. A shopkeeper chatting to Pete about the weather for several minutes could be totally unaware of Pete's intellectual disabilities, because Pete would simply fill his part of the conversation with perfectly mimicked gestures and sounds.

When his carers were told that Pete had lung cancer and had only a few months left to live, they felt that it was important he should be told this. Pete was unaware of his diagnosis, but others at Pete's day centre were beginning to speculate about cancer. 'I don't have cancer, I'm not dying like Pete, it's his own fault for smoking so much,' one woman said, even before Pete's cancer diagnosis. The staff wanted to be open. They thought that he would be able to understand what cancer was, particularly as his father had died of cancer when he was younger. However, they felt unable to break the bad news themselves; they believed that this was a doctor's task, although they were happy to support and reinforce the message.

The staff explained to the hospital palliative care consultant that they would like him to tell Pete in simple words that he had cancer. They themselves had already told Pete that he was very ill and would not get better. The consultant sat down with Pete and his care staff, and said: 'Your tests so far have shown a serious problem.' Pete responded by showing the consultant his favourite magazine, which he usually carried around and was fond of showing to everyone. The consultant decided not to tell Pete any more. He later explained: 'It was not really possible to go beyond this, as Pete was easily preoccupied with a magazine... It did not seem appropriate to go further as he did not wish to hear any further news.' His care staff, however, disagreed: 'Pete will always leaf through that magazine! He just needs to be told straight and clear.'

In the end, the care staff found a locum general practitioner (family doctor) who was willing to tell Pete his diagnosis. Pete didn't seem to grasp what was being said, but his care staff now felt that they could explain to him why he was getting so breathless and tired, referring back to 'what the doctor said about you having cancer'. The visiting palliative care nurse reinforced the information. Pete seemed to understand a little more each time and did not show any signs of distress at being told.

The consultant did a lot of things right. He didn't barge in to give Pete information for which Pete might not have been ready, or might prefer not to know. However, the problem was that the consultant was unable to assess for himself how much Pete could or wanted to understand. Pete was unable to convey this information; he would, as his carers knew, always stick to the safe topic of his magazine.

When the consultant tried to break the bad news in small chunks, he started with a 'warning shot' in order to gauge how Pete would cope with the news: 'Your tests have shown a serious problem.' However, Pete lacked the insight that this sentence, coming from a doctor, might refer to his own illness. If you had asked him what a 'serious problem' might be, he would probably have said that he'd run out of cigarettes or lost his magazine. Warning shots are often lost on people with intellectual disabilities. Talking to people with intellectual disabilities about breaking bad news, many told me:

- 'Just give it to me straight.'
- 'Don't beat about the bush.'
- 'Just come out with it.'
- 'Be clear, but kind.'

WHY DON'T THE EXISTING GUIDELINES WORK?

There are a number of assumptions underlying the existing guidelines for breaking bad news. These don't always hold firm.

Assumption 1: Breaking bad news involves one bearer and one recipient of bad news (usually a doctor and a patient)

In reality, there are many people involved in bad news situations. A clinical setting, such as the doctor's office, may be where a patient first *hears* about the bad news, but it is not necessarily where he begins to *understand* it.

In Pete's case, the consultant felt that the bad news was best broken by the care staff at this home. This is not unusual. The task of breaking bad news often falls solely on family carers and on paid care staff. In some situations, many people are involved in explaining bad news – as was the case for Pete, where in the end he was helped to understand his situation by the GP, the palliative care nurse who visited him at home, and his care staff.

Assumption 2: Breaking bad news is focused on one central piece of information

Often, the information is complex and involves a lot of different chunks of information. For Pete, the information included not only the word 'cancer' (which in itself might not mean much to some people, although Pete did have some understanding of the word), but also his increasing tiredness, breathlessness, pain, not being able to go to his day centre any more, needing to move his bed downstairs, the concept of not getting better and, eventually, of dying – and much more.

Assumption 3: Breaking bad news is a one-off event

In reality, 'breaking bad news' can be a misnomer. Bad news does not get 'broken' from one moment to the next. The GP telling Pete that he had cancer was one small event in a whole series of events aimed at helping him to understand. Breaking bad news is best seen as *a process, not an event*. It involves repetition and gradual building of understanding.

Assumption 4: Breaking bad news can be planned

In fact, any new bit of information or any change, at any time, can be experienced as bad news by someone with intellectual disabilities. All those around the person need to be constantly aware of this, always giving new information with the knowledge that it *may* become a 'bad news' situation. Furthermore, the right time for someone to learn about bad news may not be in the office of a highly trained doctor, but at home with her family or with unqualified care staff.

RE-THINKING CURRENT GUIDELINES

The current guidelines for breaking bad news were mostly developed for medical staff, particularly doctors, to be used in a clinical setting such as a doctor's office or hospital ward. This may explain in part why they don't work for people with intellectual disabilities, who often rely on others to help them understand changes in their circumstances, including changes in their health. In summary, the problems with the existing guidelines are that they:

- make assumptions about what constitutes bad news

- do not accommodate the many people involved in explaining bad news to people with intellectual disabilities
- do not give sufficient direction around the complexities of bad news situations, including ways in which complex information can be broken down and explained
- do not recognize sufficiently the gradual and unpredictable process of making sense of bad news.

These problems might also be true for the general population, but they become especially obvious when someone has intellectual disabilities. A team approach is clearly needed, with the team including family, paid carers and clinicians. This team needs to share information well, understand that the person is facing a major change in his life, and try to understand how he can make sense of such change. In the next part, I will explain my new guidelines for breaking bad news.

THINKING POINTS

Think about a situation where someone with intellectual disabilities was helped to understand bad news.

- What was the bad news? Was it just one single piece of information, or did different aspects have to be explained and understood?
- Who 'broke' the bad news to him? And who helped him to understand the news after it was initially disclosed? Was just one person involved, or several people?
- How long did it take for him to fully understand the bad news and all its implications?
- Have you ever been in a situation where you suddenly had to explain 'bad news' of any kind, without having planned or anticipated this?

PART 2

GUIDELINES FOR BREAKING BAD NEWS

CHAPTER 6

Overview of the Guidelines

The guidelines have four components, represented in Figure 6.1. There is a gradual building of someone's foundation of knowledge. At all times, you must consider: someone's understanding and capacity; all the people involved in his situation; and the support needs of everyone involved.

Figure 6.1: *Overview of breaking bad news to people with intellectual disabilities*

BUILDING A FOUNDATION OF KNOWLEDGE

This component is central to the guidelines. Gradually and over time, someone with intellectual disabilities builds his understanding of the bad news which is changing his life. The people around him can help by giving small, singular chunks of information that make sense to him. This does not have to be done simply by talking. Much of the information will be understood through experience, or in non-verbal ways, such as through looking at pictures.

UNDERSTANDING

It is essential to consider someone's capacity to understand, and the way different people understand and make sense of the same information. Some countries have laws on mental capacity that are relevant to questions around whether, how and when bad news is broken; these laws must, of course, be adhered to.

With each new chunk of information, you must decide whether the person will be able to understand it. Some people may not be able to understand certain aspects of the information at this specific point in time. If this is the case, it does not make sense to give it; rather, you should stick to the information he can understand. Of course, this is sometimes hard to assess – people may be able to understand more than we think.

In order to give people the best chance of understanding, we must consider *what and who* they need to help ensure the best possible communication, and *how* information can be given.

THE PEOPLE INVOLVED

Everyone with a significant involvement in the life of the person with intellectual disabilities should be included in the bad news situation: families, partners, friends, circles of support, paid care staff, health and social care professionals. They may all have a different but important role to play in helping someone understand and cope with the news that is going to affect and change her life.

SUPPORT

You must consider the support needed, not only by the person with intellectual disabilities, but also by the other people involved. Many will be affected personally by the bad news, particularly family and carers. They are needed to help someone with intellectual disabilities to understand and cope with the news, but in order to do so, they themselves may need help and support. This could be information, emotional support, social support, practical support and/or spiritual support. Very often, paid care staff and professionals also have specific support needs.

In the following chapters, each of the four components is explained in more detail.

THINKING POINTS

Bad news situations are usually complex. They are made up of lots of different chunks of knowledge and information. Here are some 'background questions' you need to ask:

- What is this person's capacity to understand?
- What parts of the bad news does he understand already?
- How much more can he be helped to understand?
- Is he able to understand this specific chunk of information at this specific point in time?
- What is the best way, place and time to give him the best chance of understanding the information?
- Who can best help him to understand?
- What does he need in order to communicate in the best way?
- What does everyone else need in order to be able to support him?

CHAPTER 7

Component I
Building a Foundation of Knowledge

A PROCESS, NOT AN EVENT

'Building a foundation of knowledge' is the central and crucial component of the guidelines. Our understanding of bad news does not happen in one moment. It is a process, not a one-off event, and not a series of events. For all of us, understanding has to be built gradually, over hours, days, weeks, months or even years. This means that bad news does not really get 'broken'. Usually, there is no sudden understanding of the whole situation. People understand bits of the truth over time – they may understand some of it instantly, but take much longer to understand all of it. Some people may never understand the full extent of the bad news and the impact it will have on their lives.

HELPING CARLINA UNDERSTAND
THAT HER FATHER HAD DIED

Carlina Pacelli was 36 years old and had profound intellectual disabilities. She moved into a residential care home five years ago, having lived with her elderly parents until then. Her family was close and loving; her parents, brothers and aunts visited often, and she went to see her parents at their home every other week.

When Carlina's father became gravely ill, the home manager realized that he may die and that Carlina would not be able to understand explanations in words. She took Carlina to visit him several times in hospital. When he died, the family felt unable to support Carlina, as they were coping with their own strong feelings of grief. They did not want Carlina to attend the funeral, as they felt that she would not understand what was happening. They worried that her excited noises at seeing so many familiar faces gathered in one place would upset the family. The home manager tried to explain that her staff could support Carlina at the funeral so the family didn't have to, but the family were adamant. In the end, the home manager felt that she could not go against the family's wishes at such an emotive time. With the family's agreement Carlina attended the wake, held in the Catholic church the night before the funeral, with only immediate family present. She was very excitable at the start of the wake, but became subdued after ten minutes. The atmosphere in the church was quiet and sad.

How could Carlina be best helped to understand the bad news of her father's death? It was the first time someone in Carlina's close family circle had died. Verbal explanations made no sense to her. Staff tried to talk about Dad with a sad facial expression, but Carlina, who was highly sociable and loved people talking to her, was mostly excited and pleased when they did so.

The home manager took Carlina to the chapel of rest so she could see her father's body in the coffin. When the initial excitement of the outing had subsided, she became very quiet, staring at him. She was helped to stand up from her wheelchair so she could touch her father's body. She didn't seem to understand and made it clear that she wanted to leave.

Over the next few months, the staff enabled her to visit her mother at least once a week. At first, Carlina seemed surprised that her father's armchair was empty and she seemed to be searching for him, trying to wheel her chair through the house. Staff also invited Carlina's mother to visit regularly; these visits were different from before, as her mother would never have visited without her father. As the weeks went by, Carlina became more withdrawn and often seemed lost in her own world. It took more than a year before she was back to her usual cheerful self.

When Carlina's mother died three years later, exactly the same pattern was followed. Carlina saw her mother's body at the same chapel of rest; she attended the wake (but not the funeral); she visited her old family home, now empty, one last time before it was sold; and her brothers, rather than her mother, now made the

Sunday afternoon visits to the residential home. Carlina was again withdrawn and subdued in mood for about a year. Grief has its own timetable. Her care staff felt that, this time, she was less excitable at the chapel of rest and at the wake, and seemed to grasp the sadness of the situation better.

WHAT IS KNOWLEDGE?

Knowledge is a detailed familiarity with, or understanding of, something (a situation, a person, a thing). Knowledge can include:

- facts, information and a theoretical understanding of a subject (*I know how a car engine works and I know what the road signs mean*; *I know about the physical process of dying*)
- practical skills (*I can drive a car*; *I know how to make a cup of tea*; *I can give someone a bed bath*)
- expertise (*I can judge and predict the flow of traffic*; *I know how I can make people laugh*; *I am experienced at supporting people who are sad*).

We can gain knowledge in different ways:

- education (*driving lessons*; *workshops at school about death and loss*)
- explanation (*This is how a car engine works*; *Your dad has died*)
- experience (*I am driving so fast that I can't brake in time*; *Dad is no longer at home with Mum*)
- reasoning (*I saw two accidents on the motorway, therefore motorways are dangerous*; *Dad died in hospital, and now Mum is in hospital, so that means Mum is going to die*).

We may think that 'explanation' is the crucial aspect of breaking bad news, and we may dread it. How do you tell someone that something unpleasant is going to happen? But in fact, explanations are only one way in which people begin to understand bad news. For many people, whether they have intellectual disabilities or not, 'experience' is a much more powerful way of gaining knowledge than 'explanation of facts'. Someone's unspoken reasoning can help or hinder her understanding. Education can be a good way of building a foundation of knowledge well in advance of any bad news.

Even when someone does understand the explanation, it can take time for the theoretical understanding to be turned into practical understanding and expertise. People who have lost a loved one will be aware of this. You may know in your head that the person who has died is no longer there, but it can take years for the heart to fully comprehend it. 'I keep expecting to hear his key in the front door.' When I was a hospice nurse, I found that relatives were usually shocked when their loved one died, even if they had seen the person deteriorate and had sat at their bedside for weeks. 'I knew he was dying,' they would tell me, 'but I just couldn't believe that it would really happen. It doesn't seem real.'

Verbally explaining to Carlina that her father had died was not an effective way of breaking the bad news to her. Carlina did not communicate in words, and spoken explanations were of little use. Carlina's home manager felt that seeing her father's body was the closest they could come to 'explaining the bad news', but it was only through the repeated visits to her family home that she began to comprehend the loss. Every home visit was a small contribution to 'breaking' bad news, and these were steps without words.

The acquisition of knowledge involves complex cognitive processes and is clearly affected by people's cognitive abilities: their ability to learn, communicate, associate and reason.

DIFFICULTIES IN REASONING

When Sally Burnett was diagnosed with cancer, her stepmother spent much time trying to help her understand that this didn't mean she would soon die. Sally had autism. Her stepmother explained: 'Sally's dad had cancer, and he died after twelve weeks. So she thought, "Cancer, died." Everything is black and white with her. She doesn't understand things in-between very well.'

UNDERSTANDING TAKES TIME

My son processes new information slowly, but does have a good memory. Sometimes you tell him something, and you don't think he has retained the info, but then it comes out weeks later.

'Our cat was unwell for two months, needed an operation, was kept indoors, looked after and fussed over. Then, a few days after he was finally let outside again, he was run over. My son didn't see the cat dead. When he heard the news, he laughed, despite everyone else being very upset. It seemed as if he didn't connect the information about the cat being dead with the much-loved pet. But a few weeks later, he cried at school because the cat had died. The school staff didn't understand why he was upset, so now we make sure that we let them know if something upsetting happens, and to be aware that the reaction may be very delayed.'

BUILDING KNOWLEDGE

Rather than 'breaking bad news' in one instant, we need to help people to understand and cope with a changed and changing reality. We need to help them to build knowledge. How can we do this?

Break information down into chunks

Break complex information down into singular chunks of information, and try to establish which of these the person already possesses. A 'chunk' consists of a distinct, discrete piece of information. For example:

Doctors make ill people better	My tummy hurts	I can't get out of bed	Mum is upset
Dad will have an operation tomorrow	That nurse keeps coming to my house	Staff members don't stay around	Mum decides everything for me

Some of these chunks will be 'background knowledge'; some will be about 'what is happening right now'; and some will be about 'what will happen in the future' (see Chapter 11). Part 4 of this book gives detailed case examples of how bad news can be broken down into single chunks.

Decide which new chunks of information are needed

Remember that the aim of breaking bad news is to help someone cope with a changed or changing reality. What does he need to understand in order to cope? Is he able to understand why a blood test is needed, and if so, will understanding this help him to endure the test? In the example in Chapter 1, Amanda said that she found it hard to cope with her ill mother's bad moods because she didn't understand why they happened. Amanda had the intellectual and emotional capacity to understand illness and the way illness can affect how people feel and behave. It would have helped her to know more about her mother's illness.

You will need to decide whether it is important that someone understands a chunk of information *now*. People faced with a decision about medical treatment may need information that will enable them to take that decision (see Appendix 3 on mental capacity). People whose circumstances have changed suddenly will need to be given new chunks of knowledge quickly, even if it then takes them a long time to make sense of it. This could be, for example, a sudden death in the family or an unexpected and quick move to a new residential care setting (see Chapter 18 on sudden bad news).

The size of the chunk depends on the individual

Some people can cope with larger chunks:

'We're going to drive to the hospital tomorrow, and you are going to have a blood test at the hospital.'

Others need them broken down further:

'We are going in the car.'

Later: 'Now we are driving to the hospital.'

Later: 'This nurse is going to prick your arm with a needle.'

In these two examples, we assume of course that the person has either consented to having the blood test, or – if she lacks capacity, as is likely in the second example – it was a decision taken in her 'best interest', carefully considered by the medical team, her family and others involved in supporting her.

Give new chunks of information one by one

Give the new chunks of information one by one, in order to build a solid foundation of knowledge. Additional chunks of information can be given as someone's foundation of knowledge grows. Next time she goes for a blood test, she may cope with more information presented at once.

New chunks of information need to make sense to the person

To someone whose primary way of understanding is through experience or objects of reference, explanations that she is going to have a blood test tomorrow will not make sense. She will need to see the needle in the context of being in the hospital clinic.

Telling someone why his day activity service is closing (government cuts, staffing issues) may make no sense if he lacks a foundation of knowledge about organizational and funding issues. The new chunks of knowledge will need to centre around the way in which the changes affect his life (a new place to go during the day; a different bus journey; a different routine at meal times).

Use diverse and creative ways of communicating the information

This can include:

- accessible materials: pictures, personalized calendars, easy-read information, audio materials, easy-to-use computer programs – the possibilities are endless
- pictorial scenarios, social stories and story-telling (using examples of similar changes happening to a fictional person)
- involving carers who can support someone's unique communication
- finding ways of letting someone experience the situation (e.g. arranging a visit to the hospital ward before admission to hospital).

THINKING POINTS

- What is the best way, place and time to give this person the best chance of understanding the information?

- How does she usually gain knowledge? Does she understand explanations, does she like to discuss things, does she respond well to pictures, does she learn best through experience?

- What experiences can you give her that will help her understand?

- How complex is the information you are giving her? Can it be broken down into smaller chunks? How?

- How big are the chunks of information she can cope with?

CHAPTER 8

Component 2

Understanding

DO THE RESIDENTS UNDERSTAND
THAT SOMEONE HAS DIED?

Rahim Singh was a long-term resident at a care home. When he died, nobody explained this to the fellow residents, all of whom had severe and profound intellectual disabilities. 'They can't possibly understand,' the staff argued. 'What is the point? Rahim never communicated with them anyway. They won't miss him.' It was difficult to know whether this was true. The residents could not ask questions or explain their feelings. However, it seems hard to believe that they did not notice the change. This group of residents had lived together for several decades.

In another home of people with severe and profound intellectual disabilities, staff organized a wake when John Morris died. They created a special corner where they put John's empty chair, his favourite clothes and the hand-held mirror he used to carry around with him. They put on his favourite music. The corner was kept in place for several months, and sometimes the other residents would stand quietly to look at it, mention John's name or sit down in his chair.

DOES JEMIMA UNDERSTAND THAT SHE IS DYING?

Jemima Rosing was 25 years old when she died. Her health had deteriorated gradually during the past ten years, and there had been several episodes when doctors didn't believe she would pull through. Jemima and her parents had lived with the possibility of her dying for a long time. Jemima had moderate to severe intellectual disabilities. She had a very close bond with her mother, who didn't explain to her that she was going to die, partly because the future was so uncertain and no firm information could be given. It was, in any case, difficult to know whether Jemima would grasp the theoretical concept of death.

After her death, her mother reflected: 'I do feel very strongly that, looking back over those last six months of her life, she had a very strong sense that she was dying. And there was a lot of sadness for her. She wanted to do all the things that other young people do and she couldn't do it any more. I do think that the physical change helped her to understand that the light was going out of her life.'

WHAT IS UNDERSTANDING?

'Understanding' is difficult to define. To understand something (a concept, a chunk of information or knowledge) implies an ability to make links between cause and effect. Someone understands what painkillers are if he can make the link between taking the pill and the pain going away.

'Understanding' also implies an ability to retrieve memories and making the right connections. Someone may not understand the spoken word 'painkiller' but can recognize a photograph or drawing of a painkiller. He may make the connection between the picture and the time when he himself had to take pills. Someone may tell you 'If you smoke, you get cancer', without necessarily understanding that smoking can lead to cancer. He may simply be repeating what other people have said. He may understand that smoking is not a good idea, without understanding what cancer is. Or he may indeed understand that smoking can sometimes lead to cancer, a serious illness that can lead to death.

HOW MUCH CAN SOMEONE UNDERSTAND?

We cannot always know whether someone really understands something – in fact, we usually don't. In the examples of Rahim and John, it was difficult to know how much the residents in either of the two care homes understood about death. Here are some important considerations:

- People may understand more, or less, than we think.
- We cannot make assumptions about people's understanding.
- Understanding does not only come from explanations, but also from experience.
- Even if someone doesn't understand the facts, they will still understand that something has changed.

Some new knowledge needs to be repeated regularly and often, in different contexts. When you are trying to add new 'chunks of knowledge' to someone's knowledge base, see if you can find ways of checking whether she has understood them. If she doesn't understand what you are trying to explain, it doesn't mean that she is *incapable* of understanding. It may simply be that you have not found a method of explaining that makes sense to her, and that she can't yet connect your information with the knowledge she already has.

MENTAL CAPACITY

The question of understanding is linked to the legal concept of 'mental capacity'. The laws around capacity and consent differ between countries. If the bad news situation involves information about someone's own health, and in particular if it involves care and treatment decisions, you *must* comply with these laws on mental capacity and consent. In England and Wales, it is the Mental Capacity Act 2005, which became law in 2007 and is explained further in Appendix 3.

Different cultures can have very different attitudes towards capacity and consent. Cultures also have different approaches to who can make decisions if someone is considered to be unable to make their own decisions. These attitudes and approaches are likely to influence a society's attitude towards the question of whether someone should be helped to understand bad news. If someone is not expected to contribute to decisions about their own care, treatment and future, it may be less important to help them understand. The guidelines in this book, however, are firmly based on the same principles that are behind the Mental Capacity Act in England and Wales. These principles include the following:

- There is an *assumption of capacity*. If you have not assessed capacity, you have to assume that the person has it. You cannot start taking decisions based on what is in his 'best interest' before you have assessed whether he can actually decide for himself. The same is true for understanding: you have to assume that someone can understand. You cannot base decisions around breaking bad news on the basis that he can't understand, or that it is better for him not to understand, unless you have assessed this.

- The test for capacity is *situation-specific*: can someone take *this* particular decision at *this* moment in time? This is related to the ability to understand a specific chunk of information at a specific point in time. It is possible that:
  - someone doesn't understand one chunk of information, but can understand another
  - someone cannot understand something now, but may be able to understand it in the future.

- If someone lacks capacity, decisions around what and how much he should be helped to understand should be based on 'best interest'. This includes careful consideration of the question: 'What do we think *he* would want and choose to understand if he had capacity?'

ASSESSING SOMEONE'S CAPACITY TO UNDERSTAND

You should ask yourself the following questions, and discuss them with others who know the person well:

- What is this person's level of ability? Does he have the capacity to understand this information?
- If not, can the information be broken down even further? (For example, by sticking to information about what is happening right now.)

- Have you thought of using pictures, multi-media approaches, story-telling or social stories? They can be very helpful to:
  - assess someone's capacity to understand
  - assess someone's need and desire for information
  - explain chunks of information.
- To test understanding, you could check whether someone is able to explain things back to you in some way. This does not have to be in words; it could, for example, be by using signs or pointing at pictures.
- If you are not sure about someone's capacity to understand, who can you enlist to help you assess this? Usually family, carers, friends and circles of support will be able to assist with this. Paid care staff and intellectual disability professionals are also a very useful resource.

HOW MUCH DO THE CARERS UNDERSTAND?

You also need to consider how much the carers understand, and fill in the gaps if necessary. After all, carers are crucial in helping someone process bad news. If they don't understand what is happening, it will be impossible for them to help someone with intellectual disabilities understand it.

Carers who have intellectual disabilities

Relatives or carers of someone with intellectual disabilities may have intellectual disabilities themselves. It is worth checking carers' understanding and ability to understand. You may need to get help from intellectual disability services, particularly if the family's information and support needs are complex.

THINKING POINTS

- How much do you think this person can understand?
- How can you assess his capacity to understand? Who can help you?
- How do you know he cannot understand this particular chunk of knowledge? Are you making assumptions?
- What methods can you use to try and help him understand?
- Do you know how much the carers understand? Can you help them?

CHAPTER 9

Component 3
The People Involved

WHO BREAKS BAD NEWS?

'The person best placed to break the news is one who understands the content of the news, and who can effectively communicate with the patient. This may be a doctor or nurse or care worker, or it may be more than one person, i.e. a doctor breaking the news but someone closer to the patient putting it into familiar words and phrases that the patient can understand.'

– General practitioner

'Patients with intellectual disabilities, they need it repeated several times, so a 15-minute clinical appointment will not be the best way to tell somebody. They may need that done in their own environment with the family and the care staff around, the picture books and other bits around them, to really be able to understand it.'

– Clinical nurse specialist in palliative care, hospice

NO ONE HAS THE FULL PICTURE

Nobody possesses all the possible chunks of information and knowledge. Usually, different groups of people:

- have different kinds of knowledge

- are able to identify different parts of someone's existing foundation of knowledge
- will be able to add different chunks to someone's foundation of knowledge.

FAMILY CARERS

Families may hold the following knowledge chunks:

- someone's personal history and life experience (family carers often know more than anyone else about the 'background knowledge' someone has)
- his daily routine
- how he communicates
- how much he is likely to understand
- how he usually copes with new information, change and bad news
- what might be the best time and place to break bad news
- whether he has had similar experiences before, or knows other people who have gone through similar bad news situations.

'MY SON SEEMED CALM, BUT HE WAS TERRIFIED'

'The nurses thought that my son was coping well when they explained that he needed to have an operation. He seemed very calm and he did exactly as he was told. But I could see that he was terrified. He was much, much quieter than usual. He had an operation five years ago and there were lots of complications afterwards – it was really hard for him. He couldn't understand that this operation was much simpler and that he was likely to be home again in a few days. I really had to explain to the nurses how much support and reassurance he needed, because to them he seemed absolutely fine.'

– Mother of a man with mild intellectual disabilities

INTELLECTUAL DISABILITY PROFESSIONALS AND CARE STAFF

Intellectual disability professionals and care staff may hold the following knowledge chunks:

- best practice about communication
- how to support communication
- how people with intellectual disabilities cope with abstract concepts, including concepts of time
- how to assess capacity; how to proceed if someone lacks capacity
- how other people with intellectual disabilities and their families and carers have coped with similar situations
- how to support changes in behaviour.

'WE TALKED, DREW PICTURES AND MADE MODELS'

'There wasn't much time to decide whether or not Jennifer should have bowel surgery that would leave her with a colostomy. Without the surgery, she would die, but her family and the medical team weren't sure whether she would cope with the surgery and the colostomy. They didn't think that she had the capacity to be involved in the decision and were planning a 'best interest' meeting. But I wanted to try, because I thought that with the right support, we could get Jennifer to the point of understanding and making a decision. I find that people with intellectual disabilities often surprise us with their abilities. It took an intensive week of explaining everything in all sorts of different ways. We talked, drew pictures and made models. I took her to the hospital where she could meet a patient who was willing to show Jennifer her colostomy and talked about the operation. The nurses on the ward really helped with this too. In the end, Jennifer decided that she would like to have the operation. And so far, she is coping well with her colostomy. I think it was very useful to think about what bits of information Jennifer needed to understand in order to make the decision, how we could help her understand as quickly as possible, and how we could support her in coping with the knowledge.'

– Hospital liaison nurse for intellectual disability

GENERAL AND SPECIALIST HEALTH CARE PROFESSIONALS

General and specialist health care professionals may hold the following knowledge chunks:

- facts about the illness
- likely progression and outcome of the illness
- best practice around breaking bad news
- experience with breaking bad news
- how other patients and their families and carers have coped with similar situations.

'TELLING THEM EVERYTHING WOULD BE OVERWHELMING'

'When I have to tell new parents that their baby has severe disabilities, I can see in my mind's eye what is in store for them. I have followed lots of parents through the process of supporting their disabled child to adulthood. I don't know how each individual family will cope of course, but I do know a lot more about what it will be like for them than they do at that moment. I know about the difficult road ahead, not just in the next year but in the next 20 years. I know about the physical challenges of the disability, the emotional rollercoaster, the practicalities. But I wouldn't dream of telling them all that. It would be overwhelming. You do build it up gradually. It's not just people with intellectual disabilities who need their knowledge base building up slowly. It's everybody.'

– *Consultant paediatrician*

EVERYONE IS NEEDED

It is crucial that everyone works together in identifying what new knowledge needs to be added, and how. Family, carers and paid care staff must be involved in building the necessary framework of knowledge. Everyone is needed in order to give someone with intellectual disabilities the best chance of understanding her situation, and the role of daily carers (whether paid or unpaid) is particularly important. Everyone involved should have the power to help the person with intellectual disabilities understand different chunks of information; but they should also share these with each other.

Who does he want to have with him when receiving bad news?

The easiest way to find out is to ask! For example:

'I am going to talk to you about your illness. Who do you want to be here when I talk about your illness?'

'Do you want to be here when I talk about your illness? Or do you want me to talk to your mum first?'

However, some people with intellectual disabilities may just answer 'yes' or mention the last person they saw. In this case, you will have to involve those close to him in deciding who to tell.

'Do you think he wants to be here when I explain the results of the test? Who do you think he wants to have with him when I tell him? Who usually supports him when he hears difficult news?'

'MUM SHOULD BE THERE'

'I want my mum to come with me to the doctor. Because I don't have a clue what they say to me. Completely confused what they're saying. It's stupid.'

– Man with intellectual disabilities

'If he is going to die, the doctor needs to tell him, but Mum should be there as well because Mum needs to know.'

– Woman with intellectual disabilities

Building partnerships

Sharing bad news about health is a three-way process between the person with intellectual disabilities, health professionals, and the family or carers. If there is paid care staff involved, it is a four-way process. It can become even more complex if other professionals are involved, such as social workers or intellectual disability nurses. It is important to build a partnership between all these. This is easiest if the people involved have an understanding and appreciation of each other's very different roles and different relationships with someone with intellectual disabilities.

People with intellectual disabilities often have very strong bonds with their families, especially their parents – even if the families are not involved much in their day-to-day lives. These bonds can become more apparent and important at times of significant life transitions – death and dying are the ultimate transitions. Professionals and paid care staff have a particular responsibility in recognizing and supporting such bonds, and listening to relatives' perspectives.

It is also important for professionals from different backgrounds to find out what others can and cannot offer. Do doctors and nurses understand what paid care staff are able to do and cope with, how much the care staff can explain and support someone, and what their limitations are? Do care staff know what intellectual disability nurses can help with?

THINKING POINTS

- Apart from this person, who else is affected by the bad news?
- Who are the important people in her life? Is there an obvious primary carer?
- Who will help her to understand? Who will support her?
- How can other people be included in helping her to understand? What part do they play?
- If someone lacks capacity or could be harmed by the bad news, who are the people to be involved in deciding what is in her best interest?

CHAPTER 10

Component 4
Support

SUPPORTING THE RECIPIENTS OF BAD NEWS

'I may be the one delivering the news, but I won't be on the scene when the person starts to digest the news. You need to make sure that people have the right support in place to help them cope with the news you give them.'

– Nurse, community team for intellectual disabilities

SUPPORTING THE BEARERS OF BAD NEWS

'It can be a lot to ask a carer or relative to be the bearer of bad news and so they must be supported by professionals.'

– Consultant in palliative care, hospice

EVERYONE NEEDS SUPPORT

As we have seen, there are many people involved in bad news situations, not just the person with intellectual disabilities and one bearer of bad news. Everyone will need to be supported if they are to cope with the situation themselves. Without this, it will be hard for them to support the person with intellectual disabilities.

Support will be needed, not just at the initial stages of revealing bad news but throughout the whole process. Each group of people involved in the bad news situation has different support needs. It is worth considering what these support needs are, both now and in the long term.

FAMILY CARERS

'I NEEDED A LISTENING EAR'

'What I needed was a listening ear, but I also needed to know what was happening to my daughter. I needed to know how the cancer would proceed.'

– Mother of a woman with intellectual disabilities who had died of cancer

'The kind of help I would want is someone attached to the hospital who would be there to listen to you. How you feel, what your feelings are, as well as dealing with ways of passing on the information.'

– Father of a man with intellectual disabilities

'I found it really hard when my father died. And I couldn't face talking to my son about him. My son had been so close to his granddad. I thought that if I talked about Granddad, I would be upset and he would be upset, so it was easier not to. My son understands words but he doesn't speak, so he never asked. I don't know whether I did things right. I think maybe I should have talked to my son. But I didn't know how to do it, or who to ask for help.'

– Mother of a man with intellectual disabilities

Of all the people involved, family carers are perhaps most in need of support themselves. Whatever the nature of the bad news, families are likely to be affected by it. Coping with the fact that your sister is nearing the end of her life is difficult enough – helping your sister understand and cope with this herself can be almost too much to bear. The death of your husband means that your son loses his father – how do you help him cope with his loss if you are struggling to cope with your own loss? Seeing someone you love struggle with the changes in his life can be heart-breaking.

Family carers need many different kinds of support. If they are actively involved in helping their relative with intellectual disabilities understand his situation, they need the knowledge and practical support to do so. They may need reassurance and help in understanding how people cope with bad news situations, and what the effects might be of breaking or not breaking bad news. Perhaps most importantly, they will need someone who listens to them and tries to understand their feelings, emotions, worries and thoughts.

Depending on the nature of the bad news, there will be a clear role for certain professionals to provide information. Health care professionals should give information about illness and treatment; social workers may be able to give information about moving house. However, any of the professionals involved can provide emotional and social support.

STAFF IN INTELLECTUAL DISABILITY SERVICES

'I WAS THE PILLAR OF STRENGTH, BUT I NEEDED SUPPORT TOO'

'I think that because I appear to be strong and can cope with most things, people just assume I can cope.'

– *Support worker in community team for intellectual disabilities*

'One of our residents died at home and it was a good death. However, some months later I was interviewed for a PhD study about my experiences and I spent the whole interview in tears. I had not realized the impact of the experience. Because I was the manager I was the pillar of strength for the family, other residents and staff members. I had not really looked after *me*.'

– *Manager of a residential care home*

> 'I need to talk to the family. But the doctors don't tell me everything. They only give me a little bit of information, and then they ask me to pass it on to the family... I need to know for myself, as well. I need to be able to plan things. I need to know what is happening.'
>
> – Manager of a residential care home
>
> (from Tuffrey-Wijne 2010, p.149)

It is easy to assume that staff in intellectual disability services know how to cope. They are, after all, professionals. However, many will not encounter similar bad news situations regularly, and it can worry or even frighten them. Hospital and hospice staff are used to dealing with serious illness, death and bereavement and have usually developed a way of coping, but most intellectual disability nurses and support staff haven't. This is particularly true for untrained care staff, who may be young and without much personal experience of death and loss, let alone working experience. They can be overwhelmed by worry about death: 'I hope he doesn't ask me about it'; 'I hope he doesn't die on my shift.'

Paid carers providing day-to-day support are the most likely to be asked questions. They need other professionals to give them the necessary answers. They also need to have permission to answer questions and guidance on how to do this. Nurses, social workers or speech and language therapists in intellectual disability services may be called upon to help someone understand bad news situations. They need to have detailed understanding of the bad news, so they can 'translate' this into a communication method that the person with intellectual disabilities can understand.

Don't assume that it is only family and friends who are upset. People with intellectual disabilities often make strong connections with those around them, and paid staff can be deeply affected too. They may have known the person for many years. They may feel very distressed if she faces a life-limiting illness, or has to move to a different service, or loses a parent. All staff in intellectual disability service should have support in coping with their own emotions, in a way that suits their individual needs. Their managers have a particular responsibility in ensuring that this is in place.

GENERAL AND SPECIALIST HEALTH CARE STAFF

'I AM NOT CONFIDENT'

'I am not confident enough to break the news, because I'm not experienced with people with intellectual disabilities. So I like to call in the experts, like the intellectual disability nurse, just to support me.'

– Clinical nurse specialist in palliative care, hospice

Many general health care professionals do not know how to communicate effectively with people with intellectual disabilities or how to meet their specific needs. Whilst intellectual disability staff can be fearful of the bad news itself, general health care staff can be fearful of this group of people with intellectual disabilities, or simply lack insight into their needs. However, it is clear that doctors and nurses in general health care services cannot leave it to family or paid care staff to deal with the bad news situation. General health care professionals need help, for instance, in learning how best to communicate with someone with intellectual disabilities, who to communicate with, and how to assess understanding and capacity.

The emergence of intellectual disability liaison nurses in hospitals is helpful, but if there is no such easy access to intellectual disability expertise, general health care staff will have to seek it themselves. They need to ask family or care staff for help, because such help may not be offered spontaneously. Managers can help by ensuring that general health care staff do not neglect the needs of people with intellectual disabilities.

THE NEW GUIDELINES ARE A STARTING POINT, NOT AN END PRODUCT

I hope that these guidelines are useful in practice. I see them as a starting point, the beginning of a process of discovering what works and what doesn't work in real life. They are not cast in stone, and they will hopefully be developed further by those who use them. The more people reflect on how bad news is best broken, and the more research is conducted in this area, the better.

THINKING POINTS

- What support do you need for yourself? Can you be specific about this? Do you need information, emotional support, someone to talk to, practical help? When you know exactly what you need, it is easier to find help.

- Who can you ask for help and support? It may be that you need different people for different support needs.

- Who else is involved in the bad news situation? What do you think their support needs are? Who can meet those needs?

- Are you willing and able to listen and to consider the situation from another person's perspective?

PART 3

USING THE
GUIDELINES

CHAPTER 11

How Can We Break
Knowledge Down
into Chunks?

KAREN'S FATHER HAS END-STAGE LUNG CANCER

Karen Mackenzie is 23 years old and lives at home with her parents. Her father was diagnosed with lung cancer six months ago and is now entering his final weeks of life. He wants to die at home. The palliative care nurse from the local hospice visits regularly to help manage his symptoms and to support Karen's family. The district nurse visits every day to help with his nursing care. Karen's parents are keen that Karen is as involved as possible and is helped to understand the situation. The bad news can be summed up as: *Dad is going to die.*

Bad news is never simple. The fact that Karen's father is going to die lies at the root of the past, present and future changes in her life, yet telling Karen that 'Dad is going to die' is unlikely to be enough. Knowledge about the situation, which includes the fact that he is going to die, needs to be broken down into very small chunks. This will help us to see what Karen understands already, what she needs to understand now, what she will need to understand as time (and her father's illness) progresses, and what she is unlikely to understand at all. By establishing Karen's current 'framework of knowledge', it is easier to assess which chunks of knowledge need to be added in order to build it up to a full understanding of her father's dying. It will also help us to see *when* Karen is likely to understand that her father is dying: now; when it happens; well after he has died; or never – although it is unlikely that she will never understand it at all. Even if she cannot grasp that he has died, she will probably still understand that he has gone out of her life.

Knowledge can usually be broken down into chunks that fit into these three categories:

1. Background knowledge.
2. What is happening right now.
3. What will happen in the future.

1. BACKGROUND KNOWLEDGE

Background knowledge is the knowledge someone has already. This can include knowledge, concepts or perceptions that others may think are wrong (e.g. *All dogs bite; Dad will live forever*). Background knowledge is the following:

- Knowledge about how the world works: *Mum always decides for me; Routines can change; People don't stay in their job forever; One day my time at school will end.*
- General knowledge about illness, death, our bodies, our homes, people's jobs: *Everyone dies one day; Cancer always kills you; When people grow up they leave home; Policemen help you when you are lost.*
- Knowledge about what has happened in our lives: *Grandma has not visited us for ages; My sister left home when she went to university; Lots of staff have left; Auntie Mary had cancer and she died.*
- Knowledge about how we, and other people, have been feeling: *Mum has been crying a lot; I have been feeling sick; My sister liked moving to her new flat.*
- Concept of time: *He came to my birthday party; We go to church on Sundays.*
- Our view of the world: *I trust my family; Hospitals are horrible places.*

It is easy to make assumptions about someone's background knowledge. Telling Karen that Dad is going to die assumes that:

- Karen knows what dying means
- Karen knows that everyone dies
- Karen knows that Dad has been ill
- Karen understands that the death won't happen immediately.

Here are some of the possible chunks of 'background knowledge' in Karen's situation.

Karen's family, carers and professionals need to ask: *What chunks of knowledge does Karen possess already?* The more background knowledge Karen has, the more likely it is that new chunks of knowledge make sense to her and that she will understand them.

Filling in missing background knowledge
If chunks of background knowledge are missing, those may need to be given first – if the person is able to understand them, of course.

'*You need kidney dialysis*' will make no sense to someone who has never heard of either kidneys or dialysis. '*You are ill and you need to go to hospital for treatment*' might make sense.

'*What kind of house do you want to live in?*' will make no sense to someone whose family has always decided everything for them, or who doesn't know that it is possible to move house, or what kind of houses are available.

What influences background knowledge?

How much background knowledge someone has is affected by his intellectual capacity, his life experience and his view of the world.

- **Intellectual capacity.** Someone with severe and profound intellectual disabilities may have such limited background knowledge that certain new chunks of information make no sense to her. There is no framework of knowledge to support it. She may not have a clear understanding of death, so the news that Grandma has died has little initial effect: it isn't supported by her existing knowledge or current experience. She may experience Grandma's absence, but does not (yet) understand that the absence is permanent.

- **Life experience.** Having been in similar situations before. This has a very powerful influence on people's background knowledge. Someone who has split up with a girlfriend in the past will more readily understand what is happening when his current girlfriend breaks up with him. Someone whose mother has died after an illness will more readily understand that his ill father may die too. It is worth noting that people with intellectual disabilities often have far more experience with death than their non-disabled peers. As one mother said: 'At my daughter's special school there was so much loss around. I reckon she's experienced the deaths of about ten young people.'

- **The person's view of the world**, including spiritual beliefs. Someone who does not come from a faith background may not understand what it means that 'Dad has gone to heaven'. Someone who believes that nurses always make people better may not understand that Dad is getting more ill, despite the visiting nurse. Someone who has lived in a stable family unit with all her siblings will find it harder to understand that her sister has moved away.

The impact of watching TV soaps and other TV programmes, or following the lives of celebrities, should not be underestimated. For many people with intellectual disabilities, this strongly influences their understanding of life, including heart-break, divorce, illness and death. Such background knowledge is not necessarily accurate.

When a celebrity dies of lung cancer, someone with intellectual disabilities could interpret this as being inevitably linked: smoking always leads to cancer; cancer always leads to death. Life events in popular culture can be a good opportunity to explore difficult issues with people with intellectual disabilities, turning it into a way to build background knowledge.

2. WHAT IS HAPPENING RIGHT NOW

Chunks of information about 'what is happening right now' are easiest to explain and easiest to understand. Everyone's 'framework of knowledge' will include some chunks of information about what is happening right now – even if it is just 'I am feeling hungry' or 'Someone is shouting at me'.

Here are some of the possible chunks of knowledge about 'what is happening now' in Karen's situation.

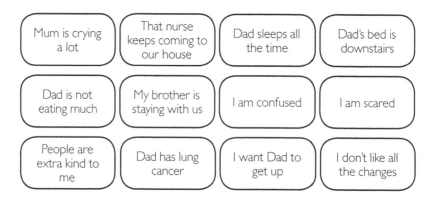

Some people, particularly those with severe and profound intellectual disabilities, have very limited background knowledge and cannot understand much information about the future. They may only be able to understand 'what is happening right now'. Complex or abstract information ('Dad has lung cancer') will be difficult to understand. To help someone with severe or profound intellectual disabilities understand new information, it has to be broken down into pieces of information about 'what is happening right now'. This means that complex information, or information about what is going to happen in the future, will be understood much more gradually, over time. The impact of the news needs to be experienced in the here and now. You can help someone understand bad news by making an effort to let her experience changes. This is what Carlina Pacelli's care staff did (Chapter 7) when they took her to see her father's dead body and helped to visit her widowed mother.

3. WHAT WILL HAPPEN IN THE FUTURE

Information about the future is more difficult to understand than information about the present. How many of the chunks of information about the future someone will understand is influenced by:

- intellectual capacity
- capacity for abstract thinking
- concept of time.

Here are some of the possible chunks of knowledge about 'what will happen in the future' in Karen's situation.

Understanding all the possible chunks of knowledge about the future will be too overwhelming for anyone, whether they have intellectual disabilities or not.

An uncertain future

Things can be particularly complicated if the future is uncertain. In Karen's situation, nobody could know exactly how long her father would live – it could be a couple of days or a couple of months. Some people can cope with an uncertain future (*We don't know when you will move house*; *We don't know what school you will go to*; *We don't know whether the treatment will work*; *We don't know when Dad will die*). But others can't, and they will need to be given only those chunks of information that are certain (*You will leave school*; *You will have treatment*; *Dad will not get out of bed any more*).

NOT KNOWING WHAT HOMES PEOPLE WILL MOVE INTO

An organization providing residential care for people with intellectual disabilities had to start the process of closing several group homes because of changes in funding and local policies on care provision, which now favoured supported-living arrangements in smaller units. The residents were helped to think about their lives, hopes and wishes for the future. However, there was no certainty about what housing might be available or whether funding would be secured for people's preferred options. At some point, it seemed that the local council wanted to reverse its policy and keep the care homes open after all. This uncertainty, difficult enough for the staff, made it very hard to know how much to explain to the residents, many of whom needed clarity and did not cope well with the drawn-out uncertainty.

How much of the future should someone be helped to understand?

In deciding whether it is important, necessary or helpful for Karen to understand some of the chunks of knowledge about the future, it will help to think through the consequences of the news for her: today, tomorrow, in a week, in a month, in a year…, and help her to understand this chunk by chunk. If she does not have a concept of future beyond a day, it may make little sense to tell her what will happen in a few weeks' time.

It is also worth considering what the consequences will be of *not* helping her understand. For example, it may be distressing to talk about funerals (even if Karen doesn't find it difficult, her parents may well find it distressing), but an opportunity to be involved in choosing the hymns and the flowers can give Karen great comfort later on and help her in her grieving process.

Remember that some people may be able to understand information about the future, but would prefer not to know – just like some people without intellectual disabilities!

I have not described the degree of Karen's intellectual disabilities, because that in itself may lead to assumptions about what she can and does understand. It is important that you consider someone's 'framework of knowledge' on an individual basis. Intellectual capacity is not necessarily the most important indicator of how much someone knows. Life experience and the way in which family, carers, paid care staff and professionals help someone understand can be just as important – sometimes more so.

THINKING POINTS

- What is the bad news, exactly?
- How can you break that down into smaller chunks?
- What background knowledge is needed for someone to understand the different chunks of knowledge?
- What parts of the bad news is she experiencing right now?
- Can you help her to understand what is happening right now? How?
- What parts of the bad news are based in the future?
- Is she able to understand knowledge chunks about the future?
- Does she want to know information about the future?

CHAPTER 12

When Can We Start Building Knowledge?

BUILDING BACKGROUND KNOWLEDGE

As we have seen, someone's existing 'framework of knowledge' determines how much and how quickly he can be helped to understand new information. In order to establish what his existing framework of knowledge is, it helps to find out:

- the amount of 'background knowledge' he has
- the accuracy of that knowledge
- how easy it is for him to retrieve, remember and use his background knowledge.

Background knowledge is built up throughout someone's life. It is never too early to start building knowledge. You can start building a solid 'framework of knowledge' well before any bad news happens. For example, in order to help someone cope with future bereavement, you could consider the following:

- death education at home or college
- taking him to visit Grandma before she dies
- attending funerals of people that are not immediate family or close friends – so that when a close friend dies, he already has some experience of funerals
- establishing rituals when pets die
- talking with friends and family who have experienced bereavement

- using events on television and in the news to discuss life events
- using a life story book.

'PREPARING MY DAUGHTER FOR MY FUTURE DEATH'

'I need to prepare Sheilagh for my own death. I am using the dog! I tell her: "Look, the dog is getting old, she may die soon." The other day Sheilagh had to go to a funeral, and afterwards I told her: "When I die I want to be cremated." But then she said: "You're not going to die yet."'

– Mother of a woman with moderate intellectual disabilities

Building knowledge takes time

Sometimes, building a framework of knowledge can take a long time. Sometimes, it can be a very painful process of learning through experience.

LEARNING THAT NOT ALL ILLNESS LEADS TO DEATH

Stefan Petrescu was a young man with moderate intellectual disabilities who lived at home with his parents. When his father developed a health problem that required regular hospitalizations for about a year, Stefan became deeply distressed, often repeating 'He is going to die! He is going to die!' His parents tried to explain again and again that his father's condition was not life-threatening, that he would come home again, and that everything would be fine in the end. It did not help: Stefan was convinced that hospitals were places where people could easily die. It was only through experiencing his father's frequent hospitalizations, and seeing that after a year his father really was well again, that Stefan was able to adjust his perception of illness and hospitals.

Anticipating future changes
Sometimes, it is possible to anticipate future changes in someone's life, and start to build his foundation of knowledge in a conscious and deliberate way. In the following example, the hospice staff knew that, one day, Patrick might need to be admitted to the hospice. They prepared him by familiarizing him with the hospice in a rather creative way.

THE LINEN TROLLEY

Patrick O'Reilly, a 59-year-old man with severe intellectual disabilities, was diagnosed with stomach cancer and referred to the palliative care team three years later. His elderly mother had already said that she didn't want him to die at home. The team started building a relationship with him by inviting him to attend hospice day care one day per week. It took several months before he started to interact with the staff and the other patients, although he enjoyed the lunches. Eventually the staff asked him to assist them by pushing the linen trolley when they replaced the bedding and towels in the hospice rooms. This was a deliberate ploy to help familiarize him with the whole hospice, and he seemed content to help. At this stage his family didn't think he understood what the hospice was – he probably thought it was just another day care centre, slightly nicer than the one he used to attend. Two years later, when he had an acute episode of pain, he was admitted to the hospice ward for a week to get his symptoms under control. Patrick had become so familiar with the ward and with the staff that he settled quickly. He had several further admissions for respite care before finally spending his last few weeks of life in the hospice.

WHAT IS THE BEST TIME FOR SOMEONE TO UNDERSTAND THE FUTURE?
Deciding when and how to help someone understand the future is a highly individual process. Some people, like Stefan in the example,

need to learn through experience – although repeated verbal explanations can reinforce that learning.

For some people, it is best to wait until 'the future' becomes 'now'. For others, it is important to understand the situation earlier, so that they can be prepared and fully involved.

Some people don't want to know beforehand that a change will happen, because it would preoccupy and worry them too much. Many, though, cope better if they are prepared. If Karen Mackenzie (see previous chapter) is never told that her father is going to die, and she doesn't expect him to die, then his death will be experienced as sudden for Karen, which can be much harder to cope with.

Remember that 'not revealing the truth' does not make the truth disappear. Ask yourself whether you really have the option of protecting someone from the truth. How are you going to support her once the truth reveals itself?

I'd like to consider two different scenarios for Karen Mackenzie.

SCENARIO 1: KAREN IS HELPED TO COPE WITH THE PRESENT ONLY

Imagine that Karen is someone who finds it difficult to cope with abstract concepts, has a poor concept of time, and copes best with facts and certainties. She can see that her father is very ill and she is distressed by the changes. His bed is downstairs in the living room, and she really doesn't like this. Beds belong in bedrooms. Karen's mother explains that Dad is too weak to climb the stairs, and that from now on his bed will have to be in the living room, because Dad will not get stronger. She doesn't explain that this will only be for a few weeks or that Dad is going to die.

Over the next few weeks, Karen is encouraged to help look after her father. As he gets weaker, the changes are put into simple words by her family and the nurses: 'Dad can't walk to the bathroom any more, that's why he needs this toilet seat by his bed.' 'Dad can't get out of bed now. He will never get out of bed again.' They also help her to understand her own emotions and those of others. One day, when she sees her mother crying and too upset to talk to Karen, the nurse explains: 'Your mum is feeling sad because she is missing your dad being well. She is sad because he will never be well again.' Later, when the nurse has gone, Karen hugs her mother and says 'I am sad.' She asks: 'Is Dad going to die?' Her mother answers: 'Yes. But not yet.' When Karen asks when Dad will die, her mother says: 'I don't know.'

The hospice nurse tells the family when the process of dying has begun. Karen's father slips in and out of consciousness and is not expected to live more than a few days. It is at this point that Karen is told 'Dad is going to die.' Karen's mother and brother spend much time at the bedside, and Karen often joins them.

Karen is at college when her father dies. Her brother comes to the college to tell her the news and take her home. She is very distressed when she sees her father, shaking him and repeating 'Wake up! Wake up!' One of the college staff, whom she is very close to, has come with her and supports her – her family is too distressed to do this.

Karen is fully involved in the funeral. During the following months, the family often talk about Dad together.

SCENARIO 2: KAREN IS HELPED TO COPE WITH THE PRESENT AND FUTURE

Now imagine that Karen is someone who is able to understand the future and usually copes best if she knows what is going to happen. In this scenario, Karen already knows that her father has lung cancer, because her family (including her father himself) and the nurses have explained this to her. When she asked, six months ago, whether Dad was going to die, her father answered: 'Yes. This cancer is very bad, and I will die of it. But I don't know when.' Her family had also explained that they wanted to make the coming months as happy as possible with Dad. Her mum had talked to her about what she liked about being with Dad, and what she enjoyed doing with him. Karen had said that she liked going to the seaside together. Therefore, they had spent a week's holiday at the seaside in the summer, and had explained to Karen that this was a special holiday because it was going to be Dad's last.

A few months before he died, Karen's father talked to her about his funeral. He asked her what hymns she liked best, and together they wrote down what he wanted. He also asked her whether she would like to have any of his things to remember him by. Karen said that she would like to have his watch, but that he should keep it until he died because he'd need to know what time it was.

When it becomes clear that her father is entering the final weeks of his illness, the nurses tell Karen (with her mother's help) that Dad is now so ill that he will have to stay in bed, and won't get better. Karen doesn't ask whether her father is going to die now, so the nurse says: 'We think that your father doesn't have long to live now. We think he is going to die soon.' Karen doesn't say anything, but later that evening she asks her mum: 'When is Dad going to die?' Her mum answers: 'The nurses don't know for sure. But they think it will be in the next few weeks.'

Karen decides that she doesn't want to go to college, because she wants to be at home with Dad when he dies. This is agreed. Karen helps her mum and the nurses look after her father, preparing drinks and buying flowers to put by his bedside.

Karen's father dies a week later with his wife, daughter and son by his bedside. Karen wears her father's watch at the funeral, showing it to all her family and friends.

We cannot say that one scenario is better than the other. In both scenarios, Karen is helped to cope with the changes in her life. How she is helped, and to what extent her 'framework of knowledge' is built upon, depends on her needs and those of her family. What made things work well was that in both scenarios:

- Karen's current framework of knowledge was taken into account
- Karen's ability to understand was taken into account; it determined both the sizes and the amounts of the new chunks of knowledge

- Karen was helped to gain new knowledge in a variety of ways – through explanations and through practical experience
- everyone helped and was involved in building Karen's framework of knowledge, including the family and the nurses
- Karen was well supported, but so was her mother.

WHICH CHUNKS OF KNOWLEDGE SHOULD WE GIVE?
Just giving the chunks *'Dad has cancer'* and *'Dad is going to die'* may not make any sense to someone, because so many in-between chunks of knowledge are missing. You cannot assume that someone with intellectual disabilities will understand the connection between the illness and something that will happen in the future, or with something that has happened in the past. For some people with intellectual disabilities, particularly those who gain knowledge mostly through experience, *'Dad is going to die'* only makes sense during the final days, once Dad's health has deteriorated considerably and he has slipped into semi-consciousness. Only then does this chunk of information fit in with someone's experience and framework of knowledge.

Is it important that someone understands the information now?
There may be good reasons why it is important for someone to understand information that is currently not supported by their framework of knowledge. This might happen, for example, in the case of the following:
- Sudden bad news (see Chapter 18).
- When there is a need to make decisions about treatment and care. The person should be involved as much as possible in making decisions that affect their lives (see also Appendix 3). If the decision needs to be taken urgently, it will be necessary to speed up the process of building knowledge, helping him to understand as quickly as possible.
- If it helps the person to understand this *now*. You may have planned with the multidisciplinary team that explanations about someone's illness can wait until sometime in the future,

but you discover that she is asking questions now. There is no harm in trying to explain things earlier, if that seems the right thing to do.

HOW MANY CHUNKS OF KNOWLEDGE SHOULD WE GIVE?

Many people cope better if they understand what is happening and are prepared for the future. We should therefore give people as many chunks of knowledge as they can handle, at a pace that they are comfortable with. However, some people cannot cope with contemplating future difficulties. It is unkind to give information that someone cannot cope with or does not (yet) want to hear.

Do not give too many chunks of new information at once. If someone asks or clearly wants to know a lot of things at once, do give the information, but make sure you repeat it in small chunks as time goes by. You can assess understanding, and the need for further explanations, by asking the person to explain things back to you.

THINKING POINTS

- Do you know what someone's existing 'background knowledge' is? Think about:
    - his life experience
    - his understanding of the world
    - his view of the world.
- Who will know about his background knowledge? How can you find out? Remember: in order to build on his existing foundation of knowledge, you have to know what it is.
- Think about the possible future changes for this person. Can you start building relevant background knowledge *now*? How?
- Do you think he needs to understand some new information *now*? Why?
- Does he cope better if he understands what is happening?
- Does he cope better if he understands what is going to happen in the future?

CHAPTER 13

Who Can Give Chunks of Knowledge?

'AM I ALLOWED TO TELL HIM?'

'I work with two friends who share a flat together. One of them, a man in his late fifties who has Down's syndrome, has been diagnosed with dementia. He has started to behave differently sometimes, pacing up and down and being very restless. He can become quite aggressive all of a sudden. He has also lost some of his skills, like making a cup of tea.

'The other day, he suddenly asked: "What is wrong with my head?" That totally floored me. I didn't know what to say. I don't know if he's been told he's got dementia, but it's hardly my place to tell him, is it? I also worry about his flatmate. We haven't told him but he is getting worried about his friend. Are we allowed to tell him that his friend has dementia?'

– Support worker, intellectual disability service

ANYONE CAN GIVE KNOWLEDGE

There can be no rules about who gives what chunks of information. Everyone involved should have a mandate to give new information as and when it seems appropriate, and to help reinforce the information that is already given. This includes not only professionals, but also paid and unpaid carers.

This means that even junior care staff need to have permission to add new chunks of knowledge. They are much more likely than a doctor to be asked questions! Family, carers and paid care staff are also in a unique position to assess how someone is processing and coping with the information, and what reinforcements or simplifications are needed.

Sharing information is essential

They can only do this, of course, if everyone shares information with each other. Everyone needs to know what someone has been told, what further knowledge might need to be added, and how the information can be reinforced. In the example of Karen (Chapter 11), her mother and brother need to know that the nurse has told her that Dad is not going to get better. They can then remind Karen of this when she is upset that Dad is not getting out of bed.

Giving knowledge is not just done by talking

A mother who takes her son to visit Dad's grave is helping him to build his knowledge of death and loss. A new member of staff who helps someone write a letter to a much missed support worker who has retired is helping to reinforce the message that the support worker has left. A nurse who comforts someone when he feels upset about not being able to walk any more is helping him to trust the messages his body is giving him – if she had jollied him along with a cheerful voice, as so often happens for people with intellectual disabilities, she would have withheld an important chunk of knowledge from him.

Knowledge is gained in many different ways. 'Giving new chunks of knowledge' is not just done in a neatly planned way by someone with professional authority.

SEIZING THE MOMENT: THE TELEVISION SOAP

The manager of a residential care home had explained to the residents that their friend had been assaulted in the street and was now in hospital. Nobody talked about this much or asked any questions, even though they were encouraged to do so. A junior member of staff was on duty when there was a similar incident of assault on a television soap. She took this opportunity to show the residents a picture book about being assaulted in the street. By watching the soap and looking at the pictures, the residents began to understand and make sense of what had happened to their friend. Ideally, the manager would have liked to give most of the knowledge chunks, but she wasn't around when the soap was aired. Luckily, the team member felt able to seize the moment.

TALKING TO THE CLEANER

'A lot of people with intellectual disabilities I've worked with have gone and spoken to the cleaner, because they trust the cleaner. And the poor cleaner is sitting there going, "OK… Right… You're asking me that… Now what do I say?!" We can't assume that because we're managers or because we're professionals, the people are going to come to us.'

– Manager of a day service for people
with intellectual disabilities

WHAT ABOUT TELLING SOMEONE ABOUT BAD NEWS FOR THE VERY FIRST TIME?

Sometimes, specific bad news is best imparted by someone who has the authority and is trusted to do so. Examples include the following:

- Information about a diagnosis or prognosis. In many cases, this is best given by a doctor in the presence of someone the person knows well and trusts.

- Sad news about a death in the family. It may be that this news is best given by a close relative, or (if the person doesn't live with the family) a manager or trusted member of staff.
- Parents divorcing. Ideally, this news should come from both parents.
- A favourite support worker leaving. This should probably come from the support worker or the manager, or both.

Regardless of who imparts the initial bad news, remember that most chunks of information will be best understood in a social context, not in a clinical setting. So even though the doctor may tell someone that he will not get better, the knowledge to support understanding of this will need to be added at home, over time.

SHARING THE INFORMATION WITH EACH OTHER

It helps if everyone shares with each other what chunks of knowledge someone has received or processed. It is worth keeping a written diary or communication book of who has said what and when. This can also include someone's questions and their non-verbal and verbal responses and behaviour. Everyone involved should be able and encouraged to use this communication book. It will make it easier for carers to refer back: 'Remember what the nurse said yesterday? Dad needs to wear that oxygen mask because he finds it difficult to breathe otherwise.'

THINKING POINTS

- Do you know what information someone has been given by others? If not, how can you find out?
- Can you think of a workable method of sharing such information with each other?
- Do you think it matters who gives certain information for the first time? If yes, who should this be, and why?
- Can you list all the people who can be involved in giving chunks of knowledge? Do they all have the skill and confidence, or do they need support?

CHAPTER 14

Who Should Be Told First?

'IF I WAS GOING TO BE TOLD BAD NEWS...'

'If I was going to be told bad news about what's wrong with me, I'd much rather a doctor told me, instead of hearing it second hand from my mum or from my dad.'

– Man with mild intellectual disabilities

'Mum should be told first. And then she can tell me. Because that's just the way it is sometimes.'

– Woman with mild intellectual disabilities

'IF MY SON WAS GOING TO BE TOLD BAD NEWS...'

'I would be very upset if I took my son to the doctor's, and the doctor broke the news with both myself and my son in the room. I know it is difficult. But a lot of people with learning disabilities rely on their mum and dad, and it is difficult if they see them upset. If my son saw me crying when the doctor told us, that would really upset him.'

– Mother of a man with intellectual disabilities

'IF I HAD TO GIVE SOMEONE BAD NEWS...'

'Who I would tell first depends on several factors. How well I, as a doctor, know the patient and my rapport with them. How well I think they will understand the diagnosis and prognosis, and their subsequent reaction to these – of course some of these are subjective and we get them wrong with an array of patients! If I, in any way, anticipated support would be needed following the discussion, I may talk with carers and family first to ensure this would be possible; ideally with both but definitely with the persons involved with daily care and support.

'I think it is important to remember confidentiality here – at the end of the day patients with intellectual disabilities can have mental capacity and we must not be paternalistic.'

– Doctor, palliative medicine

THE PATIENT'S RIGHTS AND INTERESTS

People with intellectual disabilities are not always the first to know about bad news that affects them – often, they are the last to know. Sometimes this is justified, but sometimes it is not. What if the news concerns the health of someone with intellectual disabilities? Who gets told what, when? A decision to tell someone other than himself first *must* be justified. It can only be justified if he lacks capacity or if he would be harmed by receiving the news. You have to consider the Human Rights Act and the laws on mental capacity (see Appendix 3).

This is a difficult area and there are no easy answers. Capacity can be difficult to assess, particularly if you don't know the person or have little experience of supporting people with intellectual disabilities. If in doubt, you may need help from intellectual disability professionals to assess capacity and the risk that disclosure may be harmful (see Chapter 17).

THREE EXAMPLES

Respect for someone's right to information and privacy means considering their interests first, but it doesn't mean leaving them without the support of those close to them. Here are three examples of someone with intellectual disabilities receiving bad news about their poor prognosis.

TELLING THE PATIENT FIRST, WITHOUT FAMILY OR CARERS PRESENT

'One of my clients, Michael Burton, was dying. He had a family doctor who insisted upon telling Michael himself and he wouldn't tell the carers, because he said that Michael had the right to know first that he was dying. But the carers were going to be the people who were going to support him. Michael was told but everybody else was out of the room. It was difficult, because the carers knew Michael incredibly well. They knew what he would understand. I think Michael needed them there, but the doctor wouldn't allow it.'

– *Nurse, community team for intellectual disabilities*

Michael Burton was left without support when receiving bad news, because it was thought to be his 'right' to be alone. In fact, it is poor practice to tell any patient such bad news without inviting someone close to them to be present, let alone a patient who has intellectual disabilities.

TELLING THE PATIENT FIRST, WITH FAMILY PRESENT

Angela Waight was 41 years old and had moderate intellectual disabilities. She lived in her own flat and was supported by care staff who came in several hours each day. She was well known to the community intellectual disabilities team. Her parents lived nearby and visited her every day.

Angela was diagnosed with pancreatic cancer during an emergency admission to hospital, following sudden jaundice (yellowing of the skin). Her prognosis was short; the hospital consultant thought that she only had a few months left to live. Angela's mother always accompanied her to all her hospital appointments and was at her hospital bedside for most of the day. The consultant discussed the situation with the pancreatic nurse specialist and with Catherine, the community intellectual disability nurse who knew Angela well. Catherine thought that Angela would be able to understand that she was very ill and that she would not recover. She also thought that if Angela was given the right information and support, she would be capable of making choices about her care and treatment. Catherine explained to Angela that the doctor and nurse were going to tell her what was happening with her illness, and that it would be best if both her mum and dad were there too. All three professionals were present when the doctor told Angela and her parents the results of the tests. Catherine helped the doctor to explain things in simple language. Angela's parents were deeply shocked and cried; when Angela saw this, she cried too. During the following few weeks, both nurses spent a lot of time with Angela and with the parents, together as well as separately. They explained to Angela that her parents needed to know everything about the cancer, and Angela agreed that the pancreatic nurse specialist could talk to them on their own. Catherine met with the team of care staff to explain the situation. She acted as a coordinator, making sure that everyone involved knew what was happening and how Angela had been helped to understand her situation. Despite their initial distress at Angela being given the bad news, her parents said that the openness with which they could face the situation with Angela had helped them. They believed it helped Angela too.

TELLING THE FAMILY FIRST

Bernard Fabian was 38 years old and had severe intellectual disabilities. Like Angela, he lived in his own flat close to his parents. He was supported by care staff 24 hours a day. When he was diagnosed with bowel cancer, the consultant did not think he had the capacity to understand the information. Bernard had not shown any signs of understanding what the tests had been for and had found it difficult to cope with them. The consultant spoke with the intellectual disability nurse to check his assessment of Bernard's capacity. She agreed with him. All professionals felt that Bernard would need a lot of support in order to cope with the changes in his life. The consultant and specialist nurses met with Bernard's parents to explain the situation, without Bernard present. The parents were extremely distressed and needed much support. A meeting was held with the hospital staff, the intellectual disability nurse, Bernard's paid care staff, and his parents. Bernard's support needs were discussed, including his need to understand what was happening and ways in which to give him the knowledge chunk by chunk. During the following months, Bernard's parents, who had a unique and sensitive way of communicating with him, were crucial in supporting Bernard's growing awareness and understanding. They said many times that they could not have done this without the support of the professionals from the hospital and from the community intellectual disability team.

In the cases of Angela and Bernard, the professionals thought carefully about who to tell first and had a clear rationale for their decisions. Good reasons for telling family or carers first include situations where someone:

- indicates that she prefers not to know, or asks that someone else is told first
- is unable to understand the information

- needs the family or carer to be closely involved in explaining the situation (if, for example, the family has unique ways of communicating with her)
- could be harmed by the information (see Chapter 17).

THINKING POINTS

Think of a situation where someone with intellectual disabilities was *not* the first person to receive bad news that concerned him.

- Who was told first?
- What was the reason for someone else to receive the news first?
- Was this reason made explicit?
- Was this reason justified?
- On reflection, do you think that giving the news to someone else first was the right decision?

CHAPTER 15

How Much Can Someone with Intellectual Disabilities Understand?

'I DON'T UNDERSTAND WHAT THE DOCTOR SAYS'

'The doctor says to me – and I go, "What did you say?" And then my mum has to explain it to me, what he just said. Because I don't understand, I wouldn't understand what he just said. By using the long words.'

– Woman with mild intellectual disabilities

SOME PEOPLE UNDERSTAND MORE THAN YOU THINK

'Our son communicates mainly through body language. He has some language, mostly learned responses which usually relate to singing or rhymes. He has a good level of understanding but he is never able to impress anybody when it is assessment time, so his "official" level of understanding is very low.'

– Parents of a man with severe intellectual disabilities

SOME PEOPLE UNDERSTAND LESS THAN YOU THINK

'My son is incredibly articulate. He has a huge vocabulary, but his understanding is not as good as it appears. Sometimes he uses a really difficult word, but when I ask him what the word means, he goes, "Erm…" Like many people with intellectual disabilities, he will repeat what other people have said. If you don't know him, it is easy to think he can understand more than he actually can.'

– Mother of a man with moderate intellectual disabilities

'Breaking bad news was attempted several times and always seemed to go well to those present. He would ask a few seemingly relevant questions and then say, "OK"…until the next episode when it became evident very little had been retained, or ever understood.'

– Consultant in palliative care

DOES SOMEONE UNDERSTAND MORE OR LESS THAN HE APPEARS TO?

Many people with intellectual disabilities, and in particular people on the autistic spectrum, are able to use quite sophisticated words and responses, but may not necessarily understand them. Others may understand much more than you think, but are unable to express their understanding in words. Don't assume that someone can't understand, simply because she can't tell you.

It is not unusual for people with intellectual disabilities to say that they have understood, when in fact they haven't. Many people will answer 'yes' to a question, even if the true answer is 'no'.

'YES' MAY MEAN 'NO'

'Paul's communication skills are very deceptive as he has learned that you have to make a response when asked something, but the response isn't always the correct one. Thus, when asked a question, he will reply, "Yes, I think so" or "Yes, I hope so", which may very well mean "no", and he may then be encouraged to do something he doesn't want to do. This may well result in a violent outburst.'

– Mother of a man with intellectual disabilities and autism

'I MADE ASSUMPTIONS ABOUT HER UNDERSTANDING'

'When I met Gloria for the first time, we had a very sophisticated conversation about the recent general election. Because of this, I assumed that her understanding was good on the whole. But when I had to explain the hospital tests to her, I soon realized that my explanations were too complicated. I had made assumptions about her understanding. She could discuss politics, but she had no idea how her body worked, and little understanding of cause and effect.'

– Intellectual disability nurse

HOW CAN YOU ASSESS UNDERSTANDING?

It can be particularly difficult for professionals in a clinical setting (such as a doctor's consulting room) to assess how much someone can truly understand and cope with. You may not have the time and skill to find out what someone's level of understanding really is. Help is needed from those who know him well. In the above example, it is clearly crucial to involve the parents in assessing whether Paul has responded correctly to questions. It can help to ask yourself:

Does this person understand the concepts I am trying to explain, or am I making assumptions about his understanding?

For example, someone may seem to respond well to your simple explanations that if he doesn't have the medical treatment, he will die – but does he actually understand what 'being dead' means? It is worth asking that question. 'What do you think it means to be dead?'

Using pictures can be a good way of assessing understanding with some people. Inviting someone to talk about what is happening in a pictorial situation can also identify any misunderstandings.

UNDERSTANDING CAN GO BEYOND WORDS

Someone may not understand that her mother has died, but she will certainly experience her mother's absence and miss her. Just because she can't understand or explain something doesn't mean she can't know that it is happening. People still need help in coping with the changes.

Some people may not be able to understand factual information, but they may understand the feelings in the room, the atmosphere, the body language. You do not need to hide these feelings from people, but you do have to support them in coping with it.

UNDERSTANDING THE FEELINGS IN THE ROOM

Miriam Peeters had profound intellectual disabilities. She did not understand spoken language and communicated in non-verbal ways. Miriam always responded sensitively to other people's feelings. If people felt sad, she went to sit on their lap. She became noisy and distressed when people around her were anxious or angry. When Miriam's mother died, she couldn't understand this in words, but it was clear to everyone that Miriam missed her profoundly. She would sit by the front door for hours, as if waiting for her mother to return.

THINKING POINTS

- Do you always know whether or not someone has understood?

- Can you think of examples where you have misjudged someone's understanding?

- Can you think of examples where someone understood something even though she hadn't been told in words?

CHAPTER 16

Communicating with People with Intellectual Disabilities

COMMUNICATION

A book on breaking bad news to people with intellectual disabilities would not be complete without paying attention to issues of communication. Problems with communication, even a fear of communication with someone with intellectual disabilities, are frequently given as the reason why breaking bad news was avoided, or why it failed.

Communication involves two or more people interpreting each other's language or behaviour. Most people with intellectual disabilities will have some difficulty with communication. This can include any one or a combination of the following:

• speech that is difficult to understand
• problems in understanding what is said

- problems in expressing themselves because of limited vocabulary and sentence formulation skills.

Non-verbal communication may be more important than we realize. People pick up not just what you say but, much more importantly, how you say it and how you behave.

Mehrabian (1981) analysed the emotional impact of a message. He looked at what happens if someone's spoken words don't match their tone of voice or body language. Here are his well-known statistics about how a message about feelings and attitudes is received:

- 7 per cent verbal (words only)
- 38 per cent vocal (tone of voice, silence, inflection)
- 55 per cent non-verbal (facial expressions, touch, gestures, interpersonal spacing, posture).

In other words, if there is a contradiction between your words and your behaviour, people are more likely to believe your behaviour. Such contradictions can be very confusing for people with intellectual disabilities. It is unlikely to cheer someone up if you say in a loud and jolly voice, 'Oh, don't you look well! And isn't this a lovely hospital!', but mix it with distancing and somewhat sad behaviour or worried whispering in the corner.

AUGMENTATIVE AND ALTERNATIVE COMMUNICATION SYSTEMS

'Augmentative and alternative communication' means any communication method used to support or replace speech or writing. Many people with intellectual disabilities benefit from communication aids to augment their spoken language, including:

- **objects of reference:** such as a cup to signify drinks, a towel to signify bath time
- **signs:** some sign languages commonly used by people with intellectual disabilities, such as Makaton and Signalong, use signs taken from British Sign Language together with short, simple but grammatically correct spoken sentences
- **symbol-based systems:** including photographs, line drawings and commercially available symbol packages, using communication boards or computer software

- **new technology:** this is being developed all the time; there is now an interesting range of helpful phone apps, for instance.

Health care services are becoming more aware of the need to make their information materials accessible, which is a welcome development. There can be a danger, however, that simply putting some pictures on a leaflet is considered sufficient. It is important to assess everyone's communication needs individually. Pictures can be helpful for some people, but they need to be used well in order to support your communication. It is always worth checking how someone interprets the pictures. Augmentative and alternative communication methods are an *aid* to communication, not a replacement.

Some people benefit greatly from the use of pictures that tell a story. The Books Beyond Words Series, for example, is a series of books designed to help adults with intellectual disabilities talk about difficult issues (including cancer and death), through pictorial stories of people going through those experiences (see Appendix 4: Resources).

SEVERE COMMUNICATION DIFFICULTIES

Some people have such severe communication difficulties that they do not relate easily to words, pictures, symbols or signs. Their communication needs are highly individual. They are unable to ask for things, and they are dependent on others to interpret their behaviour and needs. Their behaviour can be a reaction to others' inability to interpret their communication, and can be perceived as 'challenging'. If someone throws his food around, this might be the only way in which he can communicate that he doesn't want to eat, or it might mean something completely different. Whilst carers are understandably challenged by such behaviour, the message behind such behaviour may sometimes be indecipherable.

Breaking bad news to people with this level of communication difficulties will rely heavily on those people within their family and social circle who know and understand their communication best. It will involve mostly a validation and support of his current experiences.

USING SIMPLE LANGUAGE
No jargon or euphemisms

Using simple language may sound obvious and straightforward, but can be surprisingly difficult. I once gave a training workshop to a group of residential care staff from a home that was struggling with issues of loss – several of their residents had died in a short space of time. One of the exercises involved role-playing a scenario where the staff member had to tell someone with intellectual disabilities that their friend had died. They found this almost impossible to do. Most of the staff could hardly get the word 'dead' over their lips, instead relying on confusing euphemisms: 'He has passed away', 'He has gone to heaven', 'We have lost him'. Telling people 'We have lost Sebastian' may well lead them to wonder why we don't start looking for Sebastian.

HEAVEN IS IN HIGHGATE

Melanie Rhodes was convinced that heaven was in Highgate in London. It transpired that she was told Grandma had gone to heaven. Melanie knew that Grandma was buried in Highgate Cemetery, so her conclusion was obvious to her: heaven was a graveyard.

HEAVEN IS REACHED BY AEROPLANE

A support worker tried to be open and honest about the death of Jack Ryder's father. When she explained that his dad was in heaven, she pointed to the sky. She didn't notice that there was an aeroplane flying overhead, but Jack did. For months afterwards, whenever an aeroplane flew past, Jack looked up and waved: 'Hello Dad!'

Using simple language means 'no jargon' and using words that describe exactly what you mean. This may be counter-intuitive, as it may sound very blunt. We are used to cushioning the impact of a difficult message by the words we use. 'Grandma has passed away' sounds much less terrible than 'Grandma is dead.' 'Mum has cancer' is more difficult to say than 'Mum has a lump' (or even: 'Mum has just a little lump'). However, the importance of using straightforward language cannot be overestimated.

People with intellectual disabilities, particularly those on the autistic spectrum, may interpret language very literally. We are not always aware of the literal meaning of our words, so it is worth listening carefully to yourself and wondering how your words might be 'heard'. It is possible that even a person with mild intellectual disabilities may misunderstand terms such as 'side effect', taking it literally and believing that it affects only one's sides. An 'organ' is something you play in church; a 'stroke' is something nice you can do to a cat. Everyone misinterprets language at times, not just people with intellectual disabilities. Most people will remember mis-hearing the lyrics of songs. Not all patients will realize that a cancer doctor who says that the test results are 'positive' is actually giving them bad news.

Using only one idea per sentence

We often use complex sentences containing various ideas and questions.

> 'You need to lie on the bed and lift up your shirt so I can press your tummy to see if it hurts.'

It is much better to split these up and give the messages one by one:

> 'I want to press your tummy.'
>
> 'I want to know if it hurts.'
>
> 'You need to lie on the bed.'
>
> 'You need to lift up your shirt.'

This simple rule is easy to forget and needs constant vigilance. I once visited a woman at her flat as part of a research project. She had moderate intellectual disabilities and autism. When I asked her 'Could I use your toilet, where is it?', she looked utterly confused. It was easy to assume that she couldn't understand my words, but the problem was simply that she couldn't cope with two questions at once. Once I rephrased them, her answers were immediate: 'Could I use your toilet?' 'Yes.' 'Where is your toilet?' 'In the hall.'

CHECKING PEOPLE'S RESPONSES AND UNDERSTANDING

People with intellectual disabilities, even if they seem to have understood, may actually not have understood at all. Many people with intellectual disabilities are eager to please and will tell you what they think you want to hear.

It is also important to bear in mind that when presented with a choice, some people with intellectual disabilities tend to repeat the last option they have heard. It is useful to check out whether someone has understood by asking him to explain things back to you in their own words.

- Always check that someone has understood by asking him to explain it to you in his own words. You could say, for example: *Have I explained everything clearly? Tell me what I've just said to you.*

- People with intellectual disabilities often answer 'yes', regardless of the question. Closed questions (*Have you understood what I said? Do you have any pain?*) should therefore be used with care.

- Bear in mind that many people with intellectual disabilities tend to repeat the last option. Change your questions round to see if you still get the same response: *Tea or coffee? – Coffee. Coffee or tea? – Tea.*

- Instead of closed questions, try giving several options for someone to choose from. If someone tends to repeat the final option or say 'yes' to everything, it can help to present the options in a non-hierarchical way. You could, for instance, show someone pictures of tea and coffee – or even the actual tea and coffee – and ask him to select his preference.

'YES, YES, YES, YES'

'The doctor is quite friendly, and Sally responds. The trouble is that she nods or says "yes" to all his questions, even if I know it to be "no": Have you been sick? Have you eaten anything? Are you OK? Do you feel nauseous? Yes, yes, yes, yes.

'I stay for the physical examination. The doctor palpates her abdomen... He then tells her, speaking quickly and with a strong accent, that she will be able to eat again once she feels less nauseous, just see how it goes, try a little bit, etc etc, is that OK? "Yes," she says in strong voice, but I know that she doesn't have a clue what he talked about.'

Taken from Living with Learning Disabilities, Dying with Cancer *(Tuffrey-Wijne 2010, p.158)*

ABSTRACT CONCEPTS

Abstract concepts are more difficult than concrete ones. People with intellectual disabilities understand the things they can see and experience much more easily than those that have to be imagined.

For some people, explaining what will happen during an operation is unnecessarily complex. All they need to know is that they will get an injection that will make them go to sleep; when they wake up, there will be a tube sticking out of their skin and a drip going into their arm. This could be explained with the help of pictures on a story board. The nurses could show the recovery room and ask another patient to show their drip. The experience of an operation may be very unfamiliar, and someone may not know what a drip is.

Concepts of time

Concepts of time can be very difficult. The following sentences may be hard to comprehend:

- 'How long have you had the pain?'
- 'You need to take this tablet twice a day.'
- 'You are going home next week.'

It is helpful to mark the passing of time by using 'index events' that someone will understand; for example:

- 'Did you have the pain at Christmas?'
- 'Take one tablet with your breakfast and one tablet when you go to bed.'

MOVING HOUSE ON BOXING DAY

'One of our hospitals was closing and of course the residents all wanted to know, "When is it closing?" This was in about September, and they were told it wouldn't be until after Christmas. Just before Christmas one of the residents told me, "I'm moving on Boxing Day." I said, "Are you? Where are you moving to?" He said, "I don't know." And I said, "Well, what makes you think you're moving on Boxing Day?" And he said, "Because we were told we're going to move after Christmas."'

– Manager of a day centre for people
with intellectual disabilities

THINKING POINTS

- How can you assess whether someone is processing the new information, before adding further knowledge? Don't just ask whether he has understood: ask him to explain to you what he knows.

- Can you simplify your language? Are you using the simplest and most straightforward words? Can you break down your sentences?

- Are you sure you are only introducing one new idea at a time? Check what size of 'knowledge chunks' someone can cope with; if in doubt, keep it as simple as possible.

- Remember that words are only one small part of communication. Can you think of non-verbal ways to explain something?

- Who can help you understand his communication? Who can support you in communicating with him? His closest carers (in particular his family) will know exactly how someone communicates. Ask them to help you.

- Ask for help and advice from a specialist in intellectual disabilities. The input from speech and language therapists can be particularly valuable.

CHAPTER 17

Can Someone Be Harmed by Receiving Too Much Information?

'IF I KNOW WHAT IS GOING TO HAPPEN, I WORRY TOO MUCH'

'Jason Salford, who lives in one of our care homes, has quite a severe intellectual disability. He is always saying to us, "Don't tell me anything, I worry about it all the time and I can't do anything, I can't go anywhere, I can't live my life if I know something is coming up." Even holidays – he doesn't want to know he's going on holiday until the day he goes, because he gets so anxious that he just can't cope with it. We've had a situation where he's been going on holiday and someone told him about three days in advance. The holiday was cancelled because he got so anxious, he just couldn't go.'

– Manager, residential care service

'SHE WAS TOLD TOO MUCH, TOO SOON'

'Cecilia Watkins has end-stage renal failure. She was diagnosed with chronic kidney disease about three years ago, after a routine screening test. Just over a year ago, a well-meaning service manager told her that she was "very poorly" and that when the time came that she couldn't look after herself any more, she would have to move out of her home into a place where there was more care support. Her response was to shut her door, refuse to get dressed, and she has not left the house for eight months. She will not discuss her health with anyone. We are convinced that she thinks that if she admits to being unwell, she will be forcibly moved. We have since found out that when she was 15 years old, she was moved from her family home into institutional care, very much against her wishes. Any hint that you are trying to talk to her about her illness or about what might happen in the future, and she will cover her ears and shout and tell you to "EFF OFF". Staff have overheard her talking to herself about her illness – "No, I haven't got swollen ankles, or feet, but yes, I do have swollen thighs", and she has also been heard saying to "someone" – "No, I'm not ready yet, I'm not coming, I don't want to die yet." I just think she was told too much, too soon, and it has blocked our ability to support her, because she now won't let us in.'

– *Nurse, community team for intellectual disabilities*

SOME PEOPLE CAN'T COPE WITH TOO MUCH INFORMATION

Many people with intellectual disabilities will cope well with being helped to understand as much as possible about their situation. However, as the above examples show, some people do not want to know everything, maybe because it would make them feel too upset, worried, frightened or disheartened.

The prospect of someone being upset at bad news is not in itself a good reason for withholding it. My colleague Gary Butler, who has intellectual disabilities, once said in exasperation: 'Of course he is going to be upset! He is dying! Why isn't he allowed to be upset?' But he also knew the answer to the question why the people in our research were often not told difficult truths: 'It's because they don't know how to cope with people with intellectual disabilities being upset.'

When, then, is it right and proper to withhold some or all of the bad news from someone? How do we know how much someone should be told?

It is easiest if someone can clearly indicate how much they want (or don't want) to know. Jason explained clearly why he didn't want to know in advance that he was going on holiday. However, even this is not straightforward: when asked a question ('Shall I tell you more about it?'), many people with intellectual disabilities will respond affirmatively. It is worth testing that response, as the following example from my previous research shows.

IS SOMEONE REALLY READY FOR INFORMATION?

Vincent Sweeney was a 47-year-old man with mild intellectual disabilities who had been diagnosed with lung cancer. The prognosis was not good, but although the doctor had told him this, Vincent had not fully understood it. He lived alone and often felt lonely and frightened, lying awake at night worrying about his cancer. As part of a research study, I visited Vincent regularly for two years, until he died.

One day, I tried to find out how much he understood about his cancer, and how much he truly wanted to know. I explained that some people know about cancer, maybe because they have seen it in someone else in their family, and some people don't understand it at all. Did anyone explain it to him? 'No,' he said. Would he like to know? 'Go on then,' he said, smiling at me, as if daring me. I didn't comply immediately, because he had told me many times how confused and frightened he felt about small amounts of information that the doctors or nurses gave him. I told him that there are all sorts of cancer, and that I didn't know any more about his particular cancer than he did. But I could explain cancer in general. I asked him first what cancer meant to him, what he understood. 'Well, I know there are different kinds,' he said. 'I know someone who has got breast cancer, and that's different again, isn't it?' Should I explain it to him? I asked him this question again. This time, he answered differently. 'No, don't,' he said. 'I would only worry about it. I would be sitting here after you've gone, and think about everything you have said, and it would go round and round in my head.'

Based on Living with Learning Disabilities, Dying with Cancer *(Tuffrey-Wijne 2010, p.79)*

CAN THE PERSON *UNDERSTAND, RETAIN* AND *BALANCE* THE INFORMATION?

If someone is unable to indicate how much they want to know, it is useful to think about the test for capacity: can this person *understand*, *retain* and *balance* this information? If the answer is 'no', it may not mean that it is wrong to give the information, but it does mean that it should be given careful consideration.

Understanding the information

If someone is truly unable to understand what is being said, she probably won't be harmed if you try and explain. It is usually worth trying to explain as much as possible. It is almost inevitable that some of your explanations will not be understood by someone with intellectual disabilities. The important thing is to try and find out how she has interpreted your explanations, if at all possible; and to try and simplify the information, breaking it down in the smallest possible chunks. Sometimes, people's interpretation of your explanations may take you by surprise.

THE BODY WITHOUT THE HEAD

Shaun White, whose father had died, was told by staff that the body of his father had been buried in the ground. The staff thought that they had been explicit, clear and simple in their explanation. However, Shaun became increasingly anxious as he wondered what had happened to his father's head. It emerged that he had assumed, quite literally, that it was his father's body that had been buried, without the head.

I have been in situations where carers have spoken very freely about a person's illness and poor prognosis when that person was present. They thought it didn't matter because the person's intellectual disabilities were so severe that he couldn't understand the words. However, great care is needed in such situations:

- People may be able to understand more than you think.
- People deduct information from non-verbal clues. They may not understand the content of the spoken language, but they will almost certainly pick up body language and the emotions in the room.
- There may be other people in the room who may overhear the conversation without fully comprehending it (for example, fellow residents with intellectual disabilities).

If you are talking about someone in his presence, he should be included in your conversation even if he cannot understand your words. Sit close to him, look him in the eye (unless he dislikes eye contact, as do most people with fragile X syndrome and some people with autism), occasionally address him and (if appropriate and he doesn't mind) use touch – this will all help to prevent him feeling lonely, isolated or confused.

Sometimes, the information is simply too difficult to understand, and it may be better not to give it at all.

THE HUSBAND WHO COULDN'T
UNDERSTAND HIS WIFE'S CANCER

'There was a man with intellectual disabilities whose wife had cancer. Every single week it was like breaking bad news to him... We got a printout of the cancer information and gave it to him, and then the doctor went through the whole five pages with him. He asked a lot of questions and it was like we had done good, and he had all the answers. But the next lot of chemo was three weeks after that, and he came and asked the same questions. He looked generally in distress. It was difficult. "Do you remember when we sat and talked?" "Yeah, but I'm not sure I understood."'

– Hospital nurse

The doctors and nurses in this example had done the obvious and appropriate thing by trying to provide information when asked. However, over time it became clear that the cancer information was too much and too complex for the husband to understand, and that he was distressed. It might help him if the information was kept very simple and very short: 'Chemotherapy is medicine for your wife's cancer.'

Retaining the information

Giving information that someone won't remember is not necessarily harmful. It may be important to give it, for example, if it is needed to understand what is going on in the immediate future. However, if the information causes distress and he forgets it afterwards, there is little point (and it could be considered harmful) if it is repeated. You will need to make a decision about the importance of repeating the information. This may be the case if someone needs a lot of repetition before he understands it.

DEMENTIA

'One of our patients had dementia. His short-term memory had deteriorated to such a degree that he asked the same questions again and again: "Can't they make me better?" "No"; which led to: "Will I die?" "Yes." This caused him terrible distress again and again.'

– *Consultant in palliative care*

Balancing the information

This is the ability to understand the implications of the information. It includes the ability to put information into the perspective of 'time' and the ability to see 'the bigger picture'.

LACK OF A SENSE OF TIME

'I supported a woman with end-stage heart failure who had no sense of time. Being told that she was going to die caused her such distress, and this may have been avoided. To tell someone they are going to die can have no meaning unless it is going to happen today, tomorrow or within the week.'

– *Intellectual disability nurse*

'My son's understanding is very concrete. He takes things literally. My sister was dying of cancer, and every time I had visited her, I'd come home and he would ask, "Is she dead yet?" We had told him that she was going to die, so he asks, "Why isn't she dead yet? You told me she was going to die!" So if you told him he was going to die, he would ask: "When? What day? What time?" You can't tell him something is going to happen, and then not tell him when.'

– *Mother of a young man with intellectual disabilities and autism*

LACK OF ABILITY TO SEE THE BIGGER PICTURE

'One of our service users is part of our Management Board. She comes to meetings where we discuss what is happening within the service and make decisions about the future. This is important, but I sometimes wonder whether it is fair on her to have to cope with very complex information and worries, particularly financial worries. She became terribly upset when we discussed that the finance manager was leaving and we had to find a way to replace him. She kept saying, almost in tears: "But *who* will do his job?" We explained that we would advertise the post, but she couldn't grasp that. She wondered whether she should donate all her money to our organization, so the absence of a finance officer wouldn't lead to financial collapse. This kept her distressed for a very long time – until we had interviewed candidates for the vacant post.'

– Director, residential service for intellectual disability

If someone lacks capacity, in particular the ability to balance the information, only a limited number of information chunks will make sense (*We are going to hospital now*) but others won't (*We are going to hospital tomorrow; You will die of this illness; We need to make decisions about where you are going to live*). This is because the person lacks certain chunks of knowledge that would support the understanding, such as:

- lack of a concept of time
- lack of understanding that not everything is certain
- inability to understand abstract concepts, such as 'this unpleasant treatment will help me'.

An inability to balance the information means that the person may well be harmed by receiving it. The decisions around disclosure become 'best interest' decisions. The person needs to be supported to understand and cope with the immediate effects of the bad news. As time goes on, new information chunks need to be added to help him cope with the changing situation.

THINKING POINTS

- How do you know whether someone wants more information? If he asks, can you really be sure he wants to know the answer?

- Do you understand what information he is asking for? Are you making assumptions about the amount or complexity he wants or needs?

- Can he understand the information?

- Can he retain the information?

- Can he balance the information – put it into context and see 'the bigger picture'?

- Can he put the information into its proper time frame?

- On balance, do you think he will be harmed by the information? If so, what makes you think this?

CHAPTER 18

Sudden Bad News

A SUDDEN DEATH

Shamina Anand remembers vividly how she was told that her father had died suddenly of a heart attack. Shamina was 39 years old, had moderate intellectual disabilities and lived in her own flat. Her daily routines were important to her; this included bedtime rituals and lights out at 10pm.

'My sister rang the doorbell. I was already asleep. It woke me up. She was talking through the letterbox to say it was her. I opened the door and she said, "Dad has died." I just burst out crying. My sister said, "I am taking you to Mum's house," and we both went. Everyone was there, all my brothers and sisters and my nieces and nephews and my grandma and my aunt, but Dad wasn't there because he was dead.'

SUDDEN BAD NEWS SHOULD BE GIVEN STRAIGHT AWAY

In the case of sudden bad news, someone will need to make a big jump from one reality to another. This includes sudden bereavement or other sudden changes in circumstance.

There is no gradual way to break sudden bad news. The crucial information chunk ('Dad has died') needs to be given *immediately*, because it is needed to understand an immediate change in circumstance. There is no space and time to build gradual understanding, assess someone's concept of death or even consider her coping skills. The bad news cannot be ignored; the building of understanding and help with coping will have to come afterwards.

Sudden bad news should be given as a single and simple chunk of information:

- simple language
- no jargon
- no 'warning shots'.

For example:

'Dad has died.'

'You need to go to hospital.'

'There is no disco tonight.'

'The TV is broken.'

HELPING SOMEONE UNDERSTAND
Family, carers and professionals can help afterwards by giving the person as many 'knowledge chunks' as possible to support the understanding of the bad news. Shamina's family did this naturally, by getting Shamina to join them in their immediate family gathering and mourning. This helped Shamina to understand not just the meaning but also the impact of 'Dad has died.' It will further help Shamina if she can be involved in funeral arrangements; visit Mum who is now on her own; look at letters of condolence; see her siblings cry; share emotional support and warmth.

You will need to be prepared for frequent repetitions, maybe ad nauseam for the rest of the week – or even until next month, when the disco is happening again!

'Where is Dad?'

'He has died.'

'Dad has died?'

'Yes, he has died.'

'Dad has died?'

'Yes.'

'Where is Dad?'

'No disco tonight.'

'No disco tonight?'

'No disco tonight.'

'Is there disco tonight?'

'There is no disco tonight.'

It is likely that the full extent and consequences of the bad news will only be understood over time, as the changed reality itself becomes part of a new 'framework of knowledge'.

THINKING POINTS

- What is the bad news? How will it affect someone's life *now*?

- Will the person with intellectual disabilities perceive the sudden change in circumstances as 'bad news'? A seemingly insignificant change ('There is no disco tonight') may well be very bad news for someone, and needs to be treated as such.

- How can you give someone the sudden bad news in a simple, straightforward way? What words, tone of voice and body language will you use? Who should give the news?

- What knowledge chunks are needed to build understanding of the changed situation? How can you help someone understand sudden bad news – today, tomorrow, next week, next month?

CHAPTER 19

What If People Disagree about Breaking Bad News?

'DON'T TELL HER – IT WILL DESTROY HER'

Sarah Logan was 39 years old and had moderate intellectual disabilities. She lived in her own flat. Her family was very closely involved in her life. There was a strong family history of bowel cancer; several of her close relatives had died of the disease. When Sarah's father was terminally ill, she asked her mother and siblings, 'He is going to die, isn't he?' All her family members denied this. 'It's better if she doesn't know,' her mother argued. 'If we tell her, it will destroy her.'

When Sarah herself was diagnosed with bowel cancer five years ago, the family was adamant that she should not be told she had cancer. 'Don't use the word "cancer", they urged the hospital staff. 'Just use the word "lump". The doctors and nurses complied, telling Sarah that she had lots of little lumps in her tummy that needed to be taken out. She had surgery, chemotherapy and radiotherapy.

A year ago, it was discovered that the cancer had spread widely. This time, it was clear that Sarah would not survive. Again, the family refused to allow Sarah to be told the truth about her diagnosis, and again, the hospital staff complied. 'Her family know her best,' they said. 'They know what is best for her.' The nurses from the community team for intellectual disabilities, who had supported Sarah for many years, found the lack of openness very difficult. Sarah was asking questions and they didn't know how to answer them. When Sarah moved into a nursing home for her final months of life, it was agreed with the staff that the decision not to tell her about her diagnosis and prognosis would be reviewed if she ever asked outright. A few weeks before her death, Sarah asked the nurses: 'Am I dying?' Her question was never answered. Sarah's family had remained fiercely opposed to Sarah knowing the truth, and the staff did not want to go against their wishes. They never reviewed their communication strategy. Sarah's question was ignored. One of the nurses reflected afterwards: 'I often think about that. Sarah died in distress, and I wonder…would it have been better for her if we had told her?'

PROTECTION FROM BAD NEWS

The answer to the nurse's question is most probably 'yes'. Many of the professionals and paid carers in Sarah's situation recognized this, because Sarah was so clear in her questions and it was so obvious that the lack of answers caused her distress. If Sarah did not have intellectual disabilities, it is unlikely that the doctors and nurses would have withheld the truth from her when she so clearly wanted to know. In fact, withholding the truth from her went against her fundamental right to information. So why wasn't she told?

When I ask people to tell me about difficult bad news situations involving someone with intellectual disabilities, the most frequent scenarios are those where some of the people involved in someone's life (mostly, but not exclusively, family) did not want him to be told the bad news.

'THE FAMILY ARE GUARDING HIM'

'The family literally blocks access to him. Someone mentioned the Mental Capacity Act, and I think they are worried that we are going to walk in and tell him regardless. So now they won't let me visit; and on the ward they are always there, guarding him, making sure that nobody tells him anything.'

– Nurse, community team for intellectual disabilities

There are many reasons why people with intellectual disabilities are protected from bad news. Here are the voices of two family members who had not spoken to their relative about the (impending) death of a loved one:

'I CANT COPE WITH TELLING HIM'

'I find it too difficult to talk about Granddad. I also think that maybe talking about Granddad will bring back memories, it will be upsetting. Maybe it's better not to do that. My son doesn't talk, so it's difficult for him to express himself.'

– *Mother of a man with intellectual disabilities whose grandfather had died*

'I dread the moment when we have to tell her that her dad has died. What I dread most is face to face telling her. Her reaction. How we cope with helping her...'

– *Sister of a woman with intellectual disabilities whose father was terminally ill, and who had not been told this*

These are difficult and complex situations that need to be approached with great care and sensitivity. The family's need for support is clear in these scenarios, but the need of someone with intellectual disabilities for honesty is also clear.

BAD NEWS ABOUT SOMEONE'S OWN HEALTH

If the bad news concerns someone's own health (including news about diagnosis and prognosis), there are clear rules about that person's right to information. As one doctor said, 'The person comes first. The family are not my patient.'

The Mental Capacity Act

In England and Wales, professionals must follow the Mental Capacity Act (see Appendix 3). This states that neither professionals nor family or carers have the right to make health care decisions on behalf of another adult, if that person has the capacity to make their own decisions. It also states that all relevant information must be provided, and that all practical steps must be undertaken to give that information in an easy and appropriate way, so that the person can understand it.

In Sarah's case, it was clear that she had the capacity to understand her situation, and that the lack of information stopped her making decisions – not only treatment decisions, but also decisions about how she wanted to cope with her situation and with her remaining time. If someone indicates to a professional that she wants to understand more about her situation, and such understanding is possible, then the professional has a duty to give information.

Understanding families

If the family is opposed to disclosure, try to put yourself in their shoes. Giving bad news to someone you love, especially your own child – however old – can be extremely painful, and for some people it is impossible. The parents I spoke to before writing this book were very clear about this.

PROTECTIVE PARENTS

'I think your instinct is to protect somebody. There's that other bit that's saying, "Oh, you know, they're an adult and they have a right to know", but I think your motherly instinct overtakes you and you think, "Why give them more misery?" I feel that your overwhelming instinct as a mother has got to be to protect your children.'

– *Mother of a woman with severe intellectual disabilities*

Managing the situation

This is, of course, easier said than done if there are people involved who have strong views on the need to protect someone from bad news. Here are some suggestions for managing the situation (for 'family', you can also read 'staff' or 'anyone else who disagrees with disclosing bad news'):

- Listen to the family. Their views are important and valid. Find out what is at the root of their concerns. Are they worried that they won't be able to cope with the person's emotions? If so, can help and support be offered to them?
- Ask the family why they think their relative will not cope with the information. Has something similar happened in the past? They may be able to give you important insights into her coping strategies.
- Explain gently but firmly that you do not have a choice: you cannot withhold information if the person wants and needs it. It would go against your professional code of practice.
- Reassure the family that you will not barge in with the whole truth unless their relative is ready for it. You will only give those chunks of information that are necessary at a particular moment. However, also make it very clear that you cannot tell her lies.
- Try to explain that people usually cope best if they understand their situation. They will experience changes in their health. If the people around them insist that there is nothing wrong, this can be very confusing and upsetting.

OTHER KINDS OF BAD NEWS

If the bad news is of any other kind, there may be less clear-cut guidelines about the right of family, carers or professionals to withhold information. How about the bad news that Sarah's father was dying? The Mental Capacity Act does not cover this.

NOT TELLING A GROUP OF STUDENTS
THAT THEIR FRIEND HAD DIED

'I run a weekly group session at a college for young adults with intellectual disabilities. I noticed that one of the group members had not attended for several weeks, so I asked the group where she was. They said they didn't know and looked to the two staff members who were present. These shrugged their shoulders and said they didn't know either. There was a slightly panicked look on their faces. They were trying to catch my eye and shook their heads. Afterwards, they took me aside and whispered that the person had died, but that they had not told the group this; and they had no plans of doing so. They just hoped that nobody would ever ask and that the issue would go away.'

– Drama therapist

In this situation, the staff denied the students an opportunity to understand what had happened to their friend and to be sad about the loss. They also missed an important opportunity to build the students' foundation of knowledge about life and death, which will affect their ability to cope with future personal loss and its related emotions.

It could be argued that bad news, whatever its nature, affects people's lives, and therefore they have a right to understand it and be prepared for it. You will have to work closely with those who believe in withholding the news, and try to explain the consequences of *not* helping someone understand.

- State the obvious: not explaining the bad news doesn't make the bad news go away.
- It is likely that, at some point, the truth will manifest itself (Dad actually dies; their sister will move away to university; the care home will close). If someone doesn't anticipate this, it will become 'sudden bad news' (see previous chapter). Sudden bad news is harder to cope with, and there is a higher likelihood of complicated grief reactions afterwards.

- Ask: When do you suggest we explain things? Before, during or after they happen? How long afterwards? Breaking the bad news is never going to be easy, but will it really be easier to wait until afterwards? (Remember the example at the start of this book, about the man who was told that his father had died seven years after the event.)
- Explain that there is very strong evidence that people cope best if they understand their situation.
- Talk about the importance of trust. If someone realizes that you have been telling lies, what will that do to your relationship of trust?

USING THE GUIDELINES IF THERE ARE OPPOSING VIEWS

You have a responsibility to help someone understand their situation and build their 'framework of knowledge'. You will need to consider very carefully how to do this; what the appropriate new knowledge chunks are; and how best to help her understand new knowledge, particularly if she gets confusing and contradictory messages about this. You will need to pay particular attention to the question of whether she can be harmed by the new knowledge (see Chapter 17). You need to listen carefully to families who are concerned that their relative will be harmed by bad news; they have intimate and important knowledge of their relative's ways of coping. A decision to override the family's wishes cannot be taken lightly. If your messages contradict the family's messages, what will that do to someone? Who will she believe? You will need to find a way of supporting her in her confusion.

Part of Sarah's bad news situation was the fact that those close to Sarah were denying the bad news. This should be incorporated in her 'framework of knowledge'. Sarah may, for example, have the following background knowledge:

| Mum knows best | I trust my family | My illness looks the same as Dad's | Dad died of his illness |

In addition, she may have the following knowledge about what is happening right now:

In this situation, it seems almost impossible for Sarah not to be confused. She trusts her family; she thinks Mum knows best; yet what Mum is telling her contradicts her immediate experience of feeling close to death. You have a choice of which of these 'chunks of knowledge' you reinforce: Mum saying there is nothing wrong; or Sarah feeling that she is dying. You know what the future will hold. Sarah is right: she is dying. Reinforcing her mother's message will only make matters more confusing for Sarah; it will make her feel isolated and unsupported. Even if you feel you cannot help her understand any of the 'knowledge about the future' chunks, you should at least support her in affirming her current experiences.

'I ASKED HIM WHAT HE THOUGHT'

'One of our residents was dying of chronic heart failure. His family was so adamant that he shouldn't be told anything. And the doctors didn't tell him either. I am quite junior so I didn't feel that I could tell him either. So when he asked me, "Am I going to die?", I just turned the question around. I asked him, "What makes you think that?" He said that he felt weak and tired and he didn't feel as if he would get better. He also mentioned another resident who died a few years ago after a long illness. He said, "I feel like him." Then he asked me again, "Am I going to die?" So I asked him, "Do you think you are?", and he said, "Yes." And I said to him, "I think you may be right. Maybe your time has come. Maybe you are going to die." The strange thing is, he seemed much calmer after that. His family were furious, but I told them I hadn't said he was going to die. He had said it himself. And they could sort of see that this was true.'

– Support worker, residential care home

THINKING POINTS

- Is someone's right to information laid down in law? If so, is the law relevant to this situation?

- Reflect on the attitudes around disclosure of everyone involved, and try to understand everyone's point of view.

- How can you explain your point of view to the others? Remember that most people will 'hear' your point of view best if they also feel listened to and understood.

- Can you break down the conflicting chunks of information someone is receiving? Which of these chunks are you able to reinforce and support?

CHAPTER 20

Some Further Advice

Here are a number of general hints and tips that might be helpful when faced with a bad news situation. Some of these have been adapted from the general literature on breaking bad news to adults, teens and children, and people with intellectual disabilities.

Don't avoid the issue
Never avoid an issue for so long that the person might hear bad news from somebody else first. Bad news doesn't go away, and it is our responsibility to help people cope with it in the best possible way. That includes giving crucial chunks of knowledge at the right time – not simply hoping that someone will pick up the knowledge somewhere, somehow.

Anticipate questions
Anticipate that there may be awkward questions and be ready to answer them if you can. Perhaps think these answers through with someone else first.

Make sure you understand the question
It is easy to make assumptions about someone's question. It is useful to check whether you have understood where the question comes from. Even something as seemingly clear-cut as the question 'Am I going to die?' is not always straightforward. It could mean 'Am I going to die very soon/today?' or 'Am I going to die at all, ever?' or 'Am I going to die exactly in the same way as Dad did?' or 'Is this illness going to kill me and what is it going to be like?' In addition, we don't know what someone means and understands by 'die'. The honest answer to this simple question could therefore range from 'yes' and 'no' to 'I don't know'. To find out what someone means,

you could try asking: 'What makes you ask that question?' 'Why do you think that?' 'What do you mean?' 'What do you think?'

Anticipate a lack of questions

Anticipate that someone might ask unrelated questions, talk about something completely different or begin a distraction activity. There may be a lack of follow-up, where he doesn't seem to show any response in the following days. Do not assume he hasn't heard you or is not reacting.

Be honest

You don't have to tell someone everything you know (remember to build knowledge bit by bit), but you should not tell a lie. Do try and see your answer from the person's perspective. In the example below, the support worker would answer 'no' to the question 'Am I going to die?' This would not necessarily be a lie, because she knows that this person would interpret a 'yes' as 'it's going to happen immediately', which would be false. You must, however, be very aware of the risk that you are paternalistic – it is easy to misjudge someone's need for information.

I DON'T TELL HIM UNTIL THE LAST MOMENT

'I never tell him anything until the last minute. Even if I know a week in advance that someone is coming to visit him, I don't tell him until the last moment. Otherwise, he would ask constantly: "Where is she? Is she here yet? Will she be here when I come home?" I think if I were to tell him that he was going to die, he would think it would happen by tomorrow. We would have had endless questions: "Will I still be here at teatime?" It would be a nightmare.'

– *Support worker, intellectual disabilities*

Stick to statements that you know are true and that you believe yourself. Don't say 'You're going to live in a lovely new home and you will be very happy there' if you don't know for sure (and you won't) that he will find the new home lovely and that he will be happy. Don't get into complicated explanations of what happens after death unless you are absolutely sure that you both share the same beliefs about this.

Admit what you don't know
Never pretend that you know something when you don't. It is OK not to have all the answers – nobody does! However, if the question is important (as most questions are), see if there is anyone else who could answer it: 'I don't know. Shall we ask the doctor/the manager/ your brother about that?'

Allow feelings of sadness...
It is OK to cry and be upset. People with intellectual disabilities can be very upfront with their emotions. Distress, worry, anger, excitement and happiness can all surface very quickly, triggered by something seemingly minor. Some people cry easily and readily. It is important to allow it. Remember that it is not *you* who has caused the tears – it's the bad news. You can't, and shouldn't, prevent someone's distress, but you should offer support. Often, the best support you can give is simply not to turn away from distressing emotions, and not to try and make them better.

...including your own!
It is also important that you have space for your own emotions. Do you have someone to share them with? This could be the person with intellectual disabilities you are supporting. It can be very helpful for people to see that others have sad feelings too. It validates their own emotions and it can bring home the message that the news is bad. Vincent Sweeney, who had mild intellectual disabilities, realized how serious it was when the doctor gave him a cancer diagnosis: 'I saw my sister crying. I have never seen her cry before.'

If things become overwhelming for you, just take some time out to regain some emotional balance, and talk some more later. If it remains really difficult for you to broach the subject of the bad news without getting upset, ask others to help you. They could explain this simply: 'Mum finds it very upsetting. She is too sad to talk. She is thinking about Dad, but it is hard for her to talk about him. You can talk to me/your nurse/your sister instead.'

People have a right NOT to know

People have a *right* to know the truth, but they don't have a *duty* to know it. Denial, or simply not thinking and talking about the situation, can be a very important coping mechanism. Never force information on someone who doesn't (yet) want to hear it. Don't talk about a situation if someone clearly doesn't want to talk or think about it.

Don't overdo it

Don't talk for too long. Tell someone what he needs to know, give him a chance to ask a few questions, and leave it at that. Don't push it. Denial can be an important coping strategy. Do ask yourself, though, whether someone is ignoring the bad news because he hasn't understood – in which case you need to help him understand more; or because he is using denial – in which case you should respect his need not to think about the bad news.

Having told someone whatever it is you need to tell him, wait for him to come back to you when he is ready to hear more, or just look out for those moments when it seems right to chat about it together again. Reassure him that he can talk to you or ask you questions about it whenever he needs to – and make sure you honour this with attention and answers when he does.

Repeat the information

Repeat key information at different times and in different ways. This can be with words, pictures, experiences – anything you can think of.

Get expert advice

Don't hesitate to consult an expert if you feel you need to. Depending on the situation, ask for help from intellectual disability professionals, doctors, specialist nurses, managers or colleagues.

PART 4

EXAMPLES OF THE GUIDELINES IN PRACTICE

CHAPTER 21

Introduction to the Examples

In this part, you will find examples of three different bad news situations:

a. You are diagnosed with cancer. The prognosis is limited and there are complex treatment choices.

b. You need to move to a new residential care facility.

c. Your friend and housemate is entering the later stages of dementia.

Each example starts with a full framework showing a wide range of possible chunks of knowledge that are related to the situation. This is followed by a description of different individual situations, each with their own way of applying the framework in practice.

NOBODY HAS THE FULL PICTURE

Nobody possesses all the possible chunks of knowledge presented in the initial grids. Nobody knows the full extent of someone's background knowledge. Nobody knows the full extent of what is happening now and what will happen in the future.

This is further complicated by the fact that 'what is happening now' and 'what will happen in the future' changes continually. It means that the application of the grid is not static, but needs constant adjustment. Information that you thought was crucial for someone to understand might suddenly become irrelevant; information that you thought was something to be added in the future might become urgent, because circumstances change.

ESTABLISHING SOMEONE'S 'FRAMEWORK OF KNOWLEDGE'

In Example A, understanding that 'I have cancer' and that 'I am going to die' are only two chunks of a huge amount of information and changes. These two chunks will make little sense if they are not supported by someone's 'framework of knowledge'.

The person at the centre of the bad news situation has some knowledge chunks already. It is up to the family, carers and professionals to find out what these are. Establishing someone's existing framework of knowledge will be hugely helpful, as it will help everyone to see:

- what chunks need to be added now
- what chunks can and must be added later
- what chunks are not necessary for this person
- how big each chunk can be.

Writing down someone's framework of knowledge

Helping someone build a framework of knowledge is a team effort! The person is best supported if everyone works together and shares information with each other. It can be very helpful to write down what you think he already knows, and what you think he might need to know – now and in the future. This will also help you to see where your knowledge gaps are. Gradually building up a 'picture', as in the following examples, happens not only because you actually add new chunks of knowledge to his framework; your picture also grows *because you are building your understanding of what his existing framework is.* This will help you enormously when you try to support him through the changes in his life.

HOW TO 'READ' THE PICTORIAL FRAMEWORKS IN THE EXAMPLES

- The 'knowledge chunks' are colour coded. There is nothing deliberate or meaningful about the colour coding; it is simply for ease of reading and ease of reference.

LIGHT GREY: What will happen in the future

WHITE: What is happening right now

DARK GREY: Background knowledge

- Knowledge chunks that someone already has are *clustered together*. Knowledge chunks that need to be added are *indicated by arrows*. Sometimes, existing knowledge chunks are erroneous and need to be removed; these are indicated by an outward facing arrow.
- There is no particular order in which new knowledge chunks should be added. The coloured chunks do not indicate a hierarchy. It is perfectly alright to add 'future knowledge' before or at the same time as 'background knowledge'.

CHAPTER 22

Example A

Jeremy and Christina Have Cancer

THE BAD NEWS SITUATION: 'YOU HAVE CANCER'

Jeremy and Christina have cancer of the oesophagus (food pipe). The tumour is blocking their oesophaguses, so they can't swallow. There are two treatment options:

    a. An operation to remove the cancer. This would leave them with a permanent PEG tube (a feeding tube that goes through their skin straight into their stomach). They will never be able to eat normally again. There is a chance of around 30 per cent that this will cure the cancer.

    b. Putting in a stent (artificial tube) to unblock their oesophaguses. They will be able to eat, but the cancer will still be there, and they will eventually die from this.

I am not going to get better	I will have to make treatment decisions	I will go into hospital	Uncertain treatment outcomes
Not sure how long I will live	I have to give up my job	I am going to die	I want to keep going as long as possible
I will be able to eat again	Not sure if I can stay in my flat	I will spend more time in bed	I will have to plan my funeral
The nurse is visiting a lot	I want to go out with my friends	I am confused	I am scared
I can't eat	I have cancer	My family has come	I want to eat pizza
The doctor talks to me and my family	I am tired	I can't go to work	Routines have changed
Food goes from a tube into my stomach	Food keeps you alive	Food goes from your mouth to your stomach	My sister is crying
Cancer can be cured	My aunt died of breast cancer	I trust my family, staff and doctors	I have felt ill for a long time
Mum always decides for me	My view of the world	I will die one day	My concept of time
Not every cancer is the same	I am allowed to make choices	Cancer kills you	Routines can change

Figure 22.1: *Framework A. 'You have cancer' – a range of possible knowledge chunks*

JEREMY WILSON

Jeremy Wilson is 45 years old and has moderate intellectual disabilities. He lives in his own flat with daily support and has a job in the kitchen of a pizza restaurant, where he chops salads. He has an active social life with lots of friends and is close to his family whom he visits often. He has a reasonable concept of time and some understanding of abstract concepts, including dying. He knows cancer can kill you: his aunt died of breast cancer.

Jeremy has been very tired and has not been able to go to work for several months. He loves his food and has been very upset since he lost the ability to swallow a couple of weeks ago. He is currently fed through a tube directly into his stomach. Jeremy hates his tube and is longing to eat pizza. Until now, he has not been told that he has cancer. He has an appointment to see the hospital consultant and has been told that his family should come with him for support. His family has been told about the cancer, but not about the treatment options.

Jeremy goes to the appointment with his brother and sister. The cancer diagnosis and treatment options are explained to Jeremy by the consultant and a specialist nurse. The intellectual disability nurse (who has been visiting him at home) is there too. Jeremy can't really understand what the doctor is saying, but he knows that something serious and important is going on: he hardly ever sees his brother, and his sister is crying. Despite the unhappy sister, he quite likes being in here with the doctor and his family: it makes him feel important and cared for.

Jeremy's family do not want the operation. They think that it would be too difficult for Jeremy to lose the ability and prospect of eating altogether, and they think the odds of a cure are too low. They are aware that Jeremy should be involved in this decision if at all possible, and want him to, but don't know how to go about it.

Back home, Jeremy asks whether he is going to die like his aunt. His family explain that not all cancers are the same. His cancer is different from his aunt's. They tell him that they don't know whether he is going to die, and that the nurse will visit to help them understand what is happening.

Jeremy's intellectual disability nurse explains the options to him in several sessions, using props and drawings. Jeremy is very clear that he wants to eat. He doesn't want to go to hospital or have a feeding tube. Over the next weeks, the nurse explores with him his understanding that this means he will never get better, and that he will die of the cancer. When Jeremy says that he does not want to have the operation, his nurse asks him what he thinks will happen to him if he doesn't have it. He says that the cancer will stay in his body. The nurse asks him what will happen to him if the cancer stays. Jeremy answers that it means he is going to die. His nurse confirms that his cancer will make him more ill, and that in the end he will die. She asks Jeremy what it means to be dead. He answers: 'It means you never wake up and you go in a hole in the ground.' Over the next few days, he maintains that he doesn't want the operation. The nurse reports to the medical team and his family that Jeremy has the capacity to make this decision, and they abide by his wishes.

The intellectual disability nurse and doctors spend a lot of time supporting and explaining things to the family too. Jeremy's family reinforce the information from the doctors and nurses. With encouragement and help from the intellectual disability nurse, they start to talk to Jeremy about what matters in his life. They visit him as much as possible and invite his work colleagues and friends.

Jeremy's family find his illness very difficult to talk about with him, but they help him by listening carefully to what he wants to do with his life. Everyone involved will explain and support him as his health deteriorates. One day, when he is feeling sick, he asks his mother: 'Am I going to die?' His mother knows that Jeremy is taking medicine for his nausea, and that he will (most probably) not die yet. She rings the nurse, who visits the same day. The nurse explains to Jeremy: 'One day you will die of this illness. But not yet. You are not going to die now. But you are feeling very sick. I will telephone the doctor and ask him to help you with the sickness.'

A few months later, when Jeremy's health starts to deteriorate and he becomes too weak to get out of bed, he asks again: 'Am I going to die?' His mother has understood from the doctor that Jeremy has entered his final days. She says to him, 'You are very weak now. Your body is worn out. Yes, you are going to die.' She holds his hand with tears running down her cheeks. Jeremy looks at her for a long time, and then nods. It makes sense to him now. He dies a few days later.

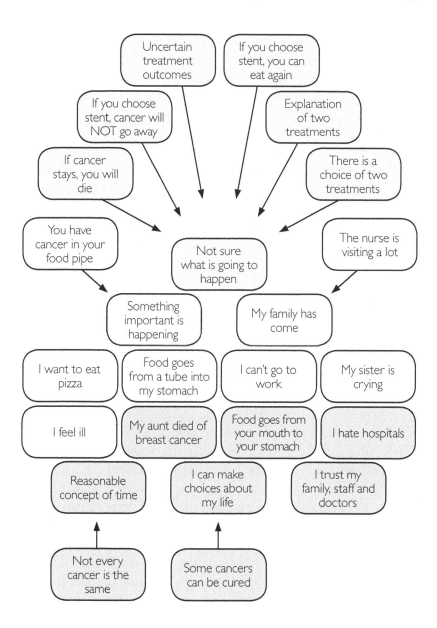

Figure 22.2: *Jeremy's current knowledge framework, with additional chunks of knowledge to be added over the next few weeks*

CHRISTINA DOHERTY

Christina Doherty has moderate intellectual disabilities and autism. She lives in a residential care home. She works in the main office of the residential care organization three days a week, fulfilling clerical tasks, which she enjoys immensely. Christina has no concept of time, and (as far as staff can tell) no understanding of cancer, or of the complexities of illness and the universality of death. She speaks and understands short, simple sentences.

Christina has exactly the same cancer diagnosis and outlook as Jeremy. She, too, is told by the doctor with her family present. She shows no sign of having understood any of the information, although she shows concern for her sister crying.

Christina's current framework of knowledge is much smaller than Jeremy's. It is not well supported and there are a number of gaps. She doesn't understand why she can't eat or why she needs the feeding tube (and hates it), and she doesn't really understand why her family has come (but likes this). She is confused and needs a lot of support to help her understand what is going on. She hates changes in routine and wants to go back to her job. She doesn't want to visit the hospital.

There are not many 'knowledge chunks' present, and it takes Christina a while to accommodate and adapt to each new one. There are a number of 'chunks' that she would not be able to understand, as they don't fit her current experience. This includes most information of what will happen in the future. She would not be able to understand that she has cancer and that she may die of this, because she cannot see the cancer and she doesn't feel as if she's dying.

However, when she is feeling particularly unwell, she asks: 'Am I going to die?' Her care staff answer: 'No, you are not going to die now. But you are very ill. You won't get better.' They realize that if they said 'yes', Christina would think that she would die very soon, and she would want to know exactly when it would happen.

The decision not to operate is a 'best interest' decision involving her family, residential care staff, hospital team and intellectual disability nurse. As time goes by, her family and staff simply add 'knowledge chunks' related to her current experiences. They don't tell her that she will have to move to a downstairs bedroom until the need for this becomes obvious to her (she can no longer climb the stairs).

Christina goes into a hospice during her final weeks of life. One day, she asks her sister: 'Am I staying here now?' Her sister says: 'Yes. You can't go home any more. You are too ill.' Christina asks: 'Am I going to die?' Her sister says: 'Yes, I think so.' This makes sense to Christina now. She shows no signs of distress and dies a few days later.

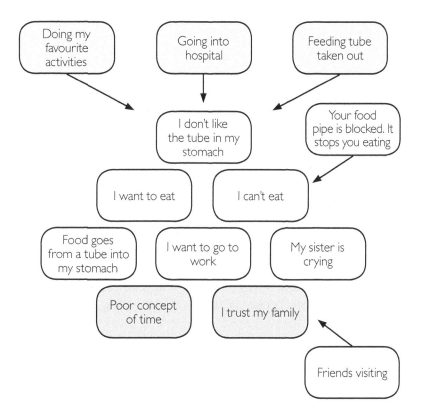

Figure 22.3: *Christina's current knowledge framework, with additional chunks of knowledge to be added over the next few weeks*

CHAPTER 23

Example B
Ahmed and Carol Have to Move

THE BAD NEWS SITUATION: 'YOU HAVE TO MOVE'

Ahmed has been living at his current residential facility for a number of years. He is happy and settled and has made a number of friends.

Carol is less happy at her current residential facility, but she knows the routines. She finds changes in her life difficult.

Circumstances have changed for both of them, and it has been decided that their homes are no longer suitable for their needs. They will have to move to a different place. They do not have a choice. Ahmed has to move in six months' time; Carol has to move within a week. Unlike Carol, Ahmed has a supportive family and a stable team of staff.

Sometime in the future, I will move again	My family will always be there for me	Not sure if I will like the new place	I will make new friends
I can still go to my family at weekends	Not sure how long I will stay in the new place	I will get used to new routines	Not sure if I will still see my friends
I will move	I will have a new bedroom	There will be new staff	Deciding what I like to keep doing
I love my bedroom	I don't want a new bedroom	I like going home	We have group meetings about moving
I am visiting a new place	I am confused	I don't understand what is happening	I like these new people
There are lots of meetings	I trust my family	I feel safe in my bedroom	My family keep talking about moving
Friends disappear from your life	Changes of environment are terrible	My friends are important to me	The staff are in charge
I don't make my own decisions	My view of the world	I won't stay here forever	My concept of time
People leave college	I am allowed to make choices	There are different reasons for moving	Routines can change

Figure 23.1: *Framework B. 'You have to move' – a range of possible knowledge chunks*

AHMED RASHID

Ahmed Rashid is 18 years old and has severe intellectual disabilities. During the week, he lives at a residential college for people with intellectual disabilities. He goes home to stay with his family at the weekends and during college holidays. Ahmed has been at the college since he was 12 years old, and will have to move in six months' time when he reaches the upper age limit of 19.

Ahmed loves his college. The staff team has been very stable. They know him well; they have helped him grow and develop, encouraging him to make the most of his many abilities. His favourite teacher is Claire, who runs music sessions – Ahmed is a natural musician and relishes the opportunity to use a wide variety of instruments.

Ahmed communicates by using single words, sounds and gestures. He has some understanding of spoken language, but sentences have to be very short and very simple. He shows no understanding of abstract concepts. His concept of time and future is severely limited: if you tell him in the morning that he is going to have a music lesson this afternoon, he goes into the music room immediately to wait for it. It helps him to have photo strips of what is happening during the day, with the Velcro-backed photos showing each event (sitting in the classroom, washing hands, eating lunch, playing outside, music lesson) which he removes as they are completed. Ahmed hates changes in routine.

A new residential home has been identified for Ahmed. His family and staff are keen that he is as prepared for the move as possible. During the next six months, they try to help him add to his 'background knowledge' by adding the knowledge that sometimes people move. At college, the staff show pictures and talk about older friends who left last year. They take Ahmed to visit some of his old friends in their new residential setting, explaining that this is now their new home. They make sure that Ahmed sees his friends' new bedrooms, which he finds very confusing. 'Wrong room,' he keeps saying. They also visit Ahmed's new residential home with him. Initially, they don't tell him that this is will be his new home, but they do introduce the residents as 'your new friends'. Staff from the new home visit Ahmed a couple of times; after a few visits, Ahmed recognizes them and is pleased to see them.

At home, Ahmed's sister is moving away to university. When his parents help her to move and settle into her new rooms, they take Ahmed along. Ahmed is very upset by the move. He keeps going into his sister's old bedroom, saying, 'Aisha gone.' He repeats 'Aisha new room' over and over during the next few weeks.

A month before the move, Ahmed's parents take him to visit his new home again, where the staff show him his new bedroom. 'This is your new home,' everyone explains. 'This is your new bedroom.' He is given a book with photographs of the home and of all the things he is going to do at the new home. Two weeks before the move, the staff at his college make a story board for him. It has a space for each day, with pictures of what is happening during the day. At the end of each day, there is a picture of his bedroom (the college bedroom during the week; the home bedroom at weekends). Day 14 shows a picture of the staff waving goodbye, the family car, suitcases, and the new home and bedroom. Every evening, Ahmed's staff or family talk through this story board with him, removing that day's pictures and anticipating the move.

The day before the move, Ahmed's family come to help him pack his suitcases. Ahmed is somewhat disturbed by this, but manages to stay quite calm. The following day, he waves goodbye quite cheerfully and is excited by the move. He immediately goes upstairs to his new bedroom, repeating 'new room' many times.

Ahmed settles in well. He particularly likes the music group on Tuesdays and Thursdays. On his wall, there is a large picture of the classmates and teachers at his old college. He often asks about them, and his father takes him to visit his old college twice. When he visits home, he is now less disturbed by his sister's empty bedroom.

Ahmed's family and staff feel that it helped enormously to have the time for preparation, when they didn't talk about his own impending move but started introducing the concept of moving. It also helped Ahmed to have the immediate future visually represented. Not everything made sense to him at the time, but the changes were less unexpected and therefore easier for him to cope with.

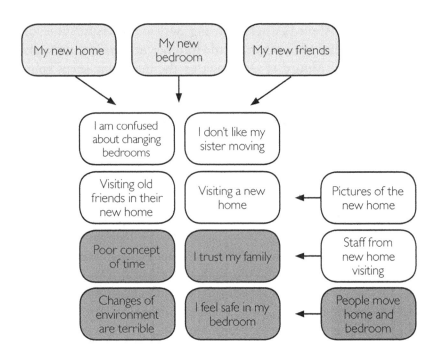

Figure 23.2: *Ahmed's current knowledge framework, with additional chunks of knowledge to be added over the next six months*

CAROL GREEN

Carol Green is 21 years old and has moderate intellectual disabilities. She has lived in her current home, together with two other residents, since leaving residential college two years ago. There is a support worker present during the day, but not at night. Carol finds life difficult and doesn't cope well with changes. There have been a lot of changes over the past two years. Only one of the support workers has remained the same; none of her housemates have stayed more than a year (their reasons for moving included living closer to the family, setting up home with a boyfriend, and moving to a nursing home due to very poor health). Carol's family live in another part of England and she has very little contact with them beyond an exchange of Christmas and birthday cards.

Carol's behaviour has become increasingly erratic. Recently, she has begun lashing out at people as well as shouting abuse at them. The staff team does not understand why and is getting very worried about the impact of Carol's behaviour on the other residents. After several meetings, it is decided that Carol's current residential care facility cannot support her needs. The team lacks the resources and skill to assess and help her. When Carol breaks the television one evening after the support worker had left, they put night staff in place on a temporary basis. A place has now become available at a residential assessment unit; this place will have to be taken up within a week.

The staff team asks the intellectual disability community nurse to help Carol cope with the rather sudden move. Carol has not yet been told that she may have to move, as she has never coped well with uncertainty, and the immediate future is not yet certain. Carol has good verbal ability and a reasonable understanding of cause and effect. On Tuesday, the long-term support worker tells her that the nurse is coming at two o'clock to have a meeting with the two of them to talk about Carol's future. At the meeting, the nurse tells Carol immediately: 'You are going to move to a new home on Saturday.' She shows Carol a picture of the new home. Carol puts her hands over her ears and shouts: 'I am not going. I am not going!' The support worker had planned to explain that there wasn't enough help for Carol at her current home, and that the new home would be better able to support her; but Carol runs out of the room and into her bedroom, banging the doors and shouting.

Over the next few days, the support workers talk about Carol's move as much as possible. They explain to the other residents within Carol's hearing: 'Carol is upset. She is going to move to a new home and she doesn't like it.' They address Carol: 'Isn't that right Carol? It is very upsetting to think about moving house. You don't want to go and you haven't chosen it.' One of the support workers offers to take Carol to go and see the new home, but Carol refuses to get into the car. Throughout the week, the support workers keep saying that Carol is moving home on Saturday.

The nurse visits every day at two o'clock. On Wednesday, she meets with Carol for five minutes before Carol storms out of the room. They look at pictures of the new home again, and the nurse explains that there are more support workers to help Carol, particularly when she is feeling angry. On Thursday, she meets Carol for 20 minutes. They look at pictures of previous residents who have left and talk about their reasons for leaving. Carol keeps pointing at one of the pictures: 'She's gone to live with her boyfriend.' The nurse asks: 'Maybe you are sad because you would like to live with a boyfriend?' Carol hugs her knees, rocks backwards and forwards and then says, 'Yes.' The support worker picks up on this theme during supper time, when the group thinks together about all the different reasons why people move home. On Friday, the nurse spends two hours with Carol. They take pictures of her room, pack her bags, and talk a lot about the sadness of moving. Carol leaves the room six times and shouts at her support worker downstairs: 'I hate you!' Finally, she sits down on her bed and cries.

On Saturday Carol keeps asking for the nurse, but the nurse is not working. Two support workers take her to the new home – Carol gets into the car quietly. At the new home, the staff give her a clear and structured timetable of events. They talk with Carol about the recent and not-so-recent events in her life; but what helps Carol most is the couple of visits from the nurse she has started to trust. Carol spends a lot of time sitting on her bed with her hands over her ears, but after a few weeks she begins to relate to the people around her in a more open way.

Figure 23.3: *Carol's current knowledge framework, with additional chunks of knowledge to be added over the next few days*

CHAPTER 24

Example C

Moira, Ben and Isabel's
Friend Has Dementia

THE BAD NEWS SITUATION: 'YOUR
FRIEND HAS DEMENTIA'

Four friends have shared a home for the past 25 years: Moira, Ben, Isabel and Jamie. They have known each other a lot longer than that, having lived in the same long-stay institution since childhood. Their current home is staffed by a dedicated team of support workers, most of whom have worked there for many years.

Jamie's behaviour has become rather strange. He used to be responsible for helping to prepare the meals and set the table and was always very good at it, but now he gets things wrong. He has started wandering into other people's bedrooms at night, switching on their lights. Recently, this usually gentle man has begun to shout at his friends.

Jamie has dementia and is now entering a stage where he needs a lot more support. His doctor thinks he won't live much longer than another year. Jamie has been told that he has dementia, and that this means it is difficult for him to think straight. Sometimes, when he gets confused, the staff explain to him that his brain is not working very well any more. He is satisfied with that explanation. He has sometimes told his friends: 'My poor brain is broken.'

Figure 24.1: *Framework C. 'Your friend has dementia'*
– a range of possible knowledge chunks

MOIRA EVANS

Moira is the most independent member of the household. She is 56 years old and has mild intellectual disabilities. She works in a garden centre four days a week and regularly brings home large bunches of flowers which she arranges beautifully around the house. Jamie has always appreciated this; he loves it when Moira puts a nice vase of flowers on the table as he arranges the crockery.

Moira has excellent verbal understanding and ability. She understands about dementia. She was close to her mother who had dementia and who died in a nursing home three years ago. At the time, Moira found it very difficult to cope with the fact that her mother didn't recognize her. However, the rest of Moira's family and her support workers did their best to help Moira understand.

When Jamie first started getting the table settings wrong, Moira just laughed at him. However, as he got more confused, she started asking questions. 'What's wrong with him?' Six months ago, the staff told her that Jamie has dementia – soon after telling Jamie himself. She is very worried about this and was overheard telling Jamie: 'My mum died you know. She had dementia and she died.' Jamie had answered: 'Well, I'm OK, it's just my brain that isn't.'

The staff spend a lot of time talking with Moira about her mother and about Jamie. They aren't sure how to explain things to Moira in a way that would help her but not worry her unnecessarily (or Jamie, as she would often tell him what she knew). They ask the community team for intellectual disabilities to help them. The nurse starts visiting regularly. Together with Moira's key worker, he explains to Moira that everyone is different, and that it may be possible for Jamie to stay at home. When she asks, they tell her that Jamie's confusion will get worse (like her mum's did), but they also tell her how she can help Jamie. Moira's key worker gives Moira the book *Ann Has Dementia* by Sheila Hollins (see Appendix 4: Resources), which uses pictures to tell the story of a woman who develops dementia. Moira loves this book; the story helps her to talk about her mother and to think about what's happening with Jamie.

As Jamie starts to deteriorate, Moira is full of compassion for him and often explains his outbursts of anger to the others. 'It's his brain, you know. He can't help it.' She takes over his task of setting the table, and is very gentle and patient when he keeps rearranging the knives and forks the wrong way. She often brings extra flowers home and puts them in his bedroom, which he loves.

As Jamie needs more support and supervision, staff numbers are increased. There is now a night sitter especially for him, to stop him wandering into people's rooms. Gradually, Jamie becomes less mobile and less able to swallow. At this point, Moira asks her key worker again whether Jamie is going to die, and her key worker answers, 'Yes, he will. We don't know when, but he will die of this illness, like your mother did.' Moira cries and says, 'I don't want Jamie to go to a nursing home.' The key worker says that she doesn't want that either, and that they are going to try their best to look after Jamie at home – but also, that there is always the possibility that something will happen to make that too difficult. Some people have to go into hospital.

Moira sits with Jamie patiently, sometimes for hours, helping him eat small teaspoons of custard and holding his hand. The staff help her by explaining Jamie's symptoms to her throughout his illness and answering her questions honestly.

Jamie dies peacefully at home, during the night. All his friends come to see him in the morning, and Moira sits with him for two hours. They are all fully involved in organizing the funeral. A year later, they still talk about Jamie a lot, missing him but also laughing at the memories.

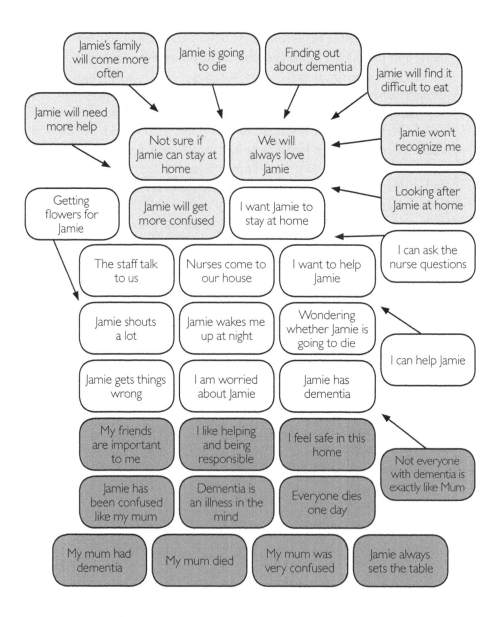

Figure 24.2: *Moira's current knowledge framework, with additional chunks of knowledge to be added*

BEN ABRAHAM

Ben is 47 years old and has moderate intellectual disabilities. He is outgoing and sociable, and has a very wide circle of friends. He is at home most days, as his day centre has recently closed. His favourite activity is the weekly disco, where he is the DJ. Ben can name any pop song he hears – the artists, the title and the year it was released. Ben's verbal ability is good, although he doesn't always show an understanding of the words he uses.

Ben is very close to Jamie. They used to share a bedroom until very recently; both have always resisted having a room on their own, as they enjoyed each other's company so much. It was only because of Jamie's recent nightly wanderings that Ben finally agreed it would be better if Jamie had his own room. He doesn't like it and misses Jamie's company.

Ben is very disturbed by Jamie's changing behaviour. He gets upset when Jamie sets his place with two knives and no fork. He looks very frightened when Jamie shouts at him. Ben has never asked any questions about Jamie. He has heard Moira use the word 'dementia' and he has sometimes repeated it ('Jamie has dementia'), but he doesn't know what that means.

Ben's key worker sits down and tries to explain to him that 'dementia' is an illness, and that the illness makes it more and more difficult for Jamie to get things right. Jamie nods, but the key worker doesn't think he has understood. She gives him the book *Ann Has Dementia* and he laughs at the picture of Ann putting a bottle of milk in the washing machine. 'Like Jamie,' he says. He carries the book around with him for several weeks, showing it to visitors: 'Like Jamie.'

The staff do not tell Ben what the future holds for Jamie, but they acknowledge and explain every change to him. 'Jamie doesn't know your name any more, because of the dementia. His brain is not working properly.' They try to encourage him to help Jamie, but Ben is often too frustrated with him. However, Ben is delighted to discover how much Jamie enjoys listening to his favourite music. One day, when Jamie is already too weak to leave the house, the staff suggest to Ben that he puts on a disco evening especially for Jamie. Friends and family are invited, and Ben relishes choosing all Jamie's favourite songs. It is clear that both Jamie and Ben love the evening.

During the following (and final) months, Ben often puts on 'Jamie's music' for him.

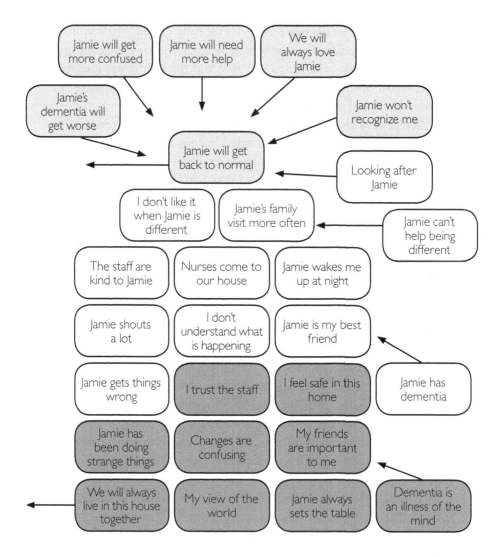

Figure 24.3: *Ben's current knowledge framework, with additional chunks of knowledge to be added*

When it is clear that Jamie is entering the final days of life, the staff tell Ben that his friend is dying. Ben reacts to this quite calmly. The staff aren't sure whether he has understood. When Jamie has died, Ben gets a CD to put into Jamie's CD player and turns it up loud.

It is Jamie's absolute favourite. 'Jamie will want to hear this when he goes into heaven,' Ben explains.

A year later, Ben still talks about Jamie almost every day. He has his photograph on his bedside table. 'I miss Jamie, I do,' he says. The staff answer: 'Yes, you do. You were best friends.'

ISABEL ALMARAZ

Isabel has always been the centre of calm in the household. She is 60 years old and has profound intellectual disabilities. She does not use words and communicates through facial expressions (smiles, mostly) and sounds. She needs much physical care, including help with moving and feeding. Because Isabel often needs the help and attention of staff, her housemates tend to congregate around her when they want to share their news with the staff. Moira adores Isabel and is very caring towards her; Isabel always shouts in delight when Moira walks into the room.

Isabel shows no understanding of Jamie's condition, and the staff don't think they can explain it to her in any meaningful way. Most of the changes in Jamie seem to go unnoticed, including the disorganized table settings or, later on, the fact that Jamie doesn't recognize his friends. Isabel has no concept of the future and experiences the present in a very immediate way. She does notice Jamie shouting and expresses distress at this. The staff help her by talking to her gently when this happens.

The staff team feels that the best way to support Isabel is by letting her experience the gradual changes in the household (including increased staffing levels and, eventually, Jamie becoming chair- and bed-bound) without explaining them in words. They don't hide the changes from her. When Jamie is bed-bound, they sometimes wheel Isabel's chair into his bedroom and stay there for a while.

When Jamie dies, Isabel is encouraged to see and touch his body. She attends the funeral. During the following weeks, staff often take her to sit in Jamie's empty bedroom. When a new resident moves in, Isabel shows some signs of distress, but this settles down after a few months. It is difficult to know how much Isabel understands about what has happened, but staff always include her in conversations about Jamie.

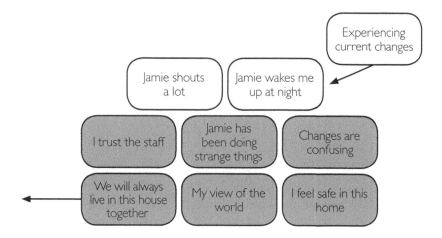

Figure 24.4: *Isabel's current knowledge framework. As she has no concept of the future, additional 'knowledge of what will happen in the future' can only be added once it becomes 'knowledge of the present'*

PART 5

APPENDICES

Appendix I

BRIEF OVERVIEW OF
THE GUIDELINES

Building a foundation of knowledge

- Break complex information down into singular, discrete chunks (or pieces) of information. A seemingly simple statement (e.g. 'Mum has cancer') usually encapsulates a vast range of background knowledge, as well as knowledge about immediate and future changes and implications.
- The size of the chunk depends on the person. Some people can cope with larger ones; others need them broken down further.
- Give the person these chunks of information one by one, in order to build a solid foundation of knowledge. Additional information can be given as the person's foundation of knowledge grows.
- Consider what 'background knowledge' the person possesses already. This will depend on his life experience and world view as well as their intellectual capacity.
- New information needs to make sense to the person. To someone whose primary way of understanding is through experience or objects of reference, verbal explanations will not make sense. People with severe cognitive limitations may never be able to understand the future.
- Decide whether it is important that the person understands this information *now*. This could be the case if he needs to be involved in treatment decisions, or if the information is related to immediate changes.

Understanding

- Assess the person's mental capacity. Capacity depends on understanding, taking on board and retaining relevant information for long enough to make the particular decision.
- Local/national legislation must be followed. Practitioners must understand how this applies to the person's situation.
- There is an assumption of capacity.
- How much someone is able to understand at a particular point influences decisions around when and how to impart what aspects of the bad news.
- People with capacity will still need to be given information in chunks, suited to their way of processing information.

The people involved

- Establish who is involved in, or affected by, the bad news situation ('stakeholders'). This can include family, partners, friends, paid care staff and health and social care professionals.
- Establish what each stakeholder knows about the person's current knowledge framework.
- Establish what knowledge chunks each stakeholder holds. This may include knowledge about the illness and prognosis, or the person's life history, understanding and communication.
- Establish who is best placed to impart and help the person process new chunks of knowledge.

Support

Establish the support needs, and the person(s) best placed to provide that support, of:

- the person
- all stakeholders, including family, friends, carers and professionals.

Support can be informational, emotional, practical, social and/or spiritual.

TEN GUIDING QUESTIONS

1. Does the person have capacity?

- Yes: Check his preference on receiving the news. Give him the diagnosis and related chunks of bad news. Follow the guidelines to support understanding of the implications, including treatment and prognosis.
- No: Discuss with carers and professionals how best to build understanding. Follow the guidelines to build understanding. Carers may be told first, but check with intellectual disability professionals before doing so.
- Not sure: Ask intellectual disability professionals to help assess capacity.

2. What knowledge does he possess already?

- Gather this information from himself, carers and colleagues.
- Someone's existing 'foundation of knowledge' is affected by:
  - intellectual capacity
  - life experience
  - world view.

3. What size are the knowledge chunks he can cope with?

- Many people with intellectual disabilities can only cope with one new idea at a time.
- Never give more than one idea per sentence. Allow time for the information to be processed.
- The size of knowledge chunks people can process depends mostly on their intellectual capacity.

- Ask family carers, paid carers and intellectual disability professionals how large the chunks of information can be for this person.

4. How many more chunks of knowledge can he be helped to understand?

- Ask the opinion of family carers, paid carers and intellectual disability professionals.
- Be guided by carers' *knowledge* of the person, rather than their *wishes*. Some carers may be protective: assess whether protection from disclosure is in his best interest.
- Knowledge can be built over time; some knowledge chunks take months to understand and need continuous reinforcement.

5. Is he able to understand this specific chunk of information at this point in time?

- Any new information or knowledge only makes sense to him if it is supported by an existing 'foundation of knowledge'.
- If he is unable to understand something now, he may be able to understand it in the future.
- It is usually best to start with the facts of what is happening now, and build understanding of the implications.

6. Is it important that he understands this specific information NOW?

- People with capacity should be involved in treatment and care decisions; they need to understand.
- Refer to the Mental Capacity Act 2005 (England and Wales).
- Ask for help from intellectual disability experts if urgent understanding is needed.
- In case of sudden changes in someone's situation, he needs to be helped to understand what is happening as quickly as possible.

7. What is the best way/place/time to give the person the best chance of understanding?

- The consultation room may be where someone first *hears* the news, but it may not be where he begins to *understand* it.
- Many people with intellectual disabilities understand new information through experience, in their own social context.
- Carers must have good information if they are to help someone understand.

8. Who can best help him to understand?

- People that he trusts.
- People who are able to communicate well with him.
- Consider both health professionals in your clinical setting (e.g. specialist nurses; speech and language therapists) and family or care staff in the home setting. All should have a mandate to add or reinforce chunks of knowledge at the appropriate times.

9. What and who does he need in order to communicate in the best way?

- Are there family or other carers who can help him to communicate? Some people with intellectual disabilities rely heavily on a specific carer for this.
- Consider the use of accessible materials (pictures, easy-read information and other audio-visual materials) and story-telling.

10. Can he be harmed by receiving this chunk of knowledge at this point in time?

- Most people cope best if they understand what is happening.
- Can he *retain* and *balance* the information? If not, he MAY be harmed by receiving it: discuss this with intellectual disability professionals and carers.
- Consider his concept of time and capacity for abstract thinking.

Appendix 3

THE MENTAL CAPACITY ACT

The law on mental capacity and consent varies between countries. In England and Wales there is the Mental Capacity Act 2005. The legal framework in Scotland is defined by the Adults with Incapacity (Scotland) Act 2000. In Northern Ireland, where there is no equivalent legislation, mental capacity issues are dealt with under common law. When considering how much information to disclose and explain to someone with intellectual disabilities, you must be sure that you act within that law. The discussion here focuses on the law in England and Wales.

England and Wales: The Mental Capacity Act 2005
In England and Wales, the Mental Capacity Act 2005 covers medical decision making. It put into law what was previously already regarded as best practice. The Mental Capacity Act stipulates that neither professionals nor family or carers have the right to make health care decisions on behalf of an adult, if that person has the capacity to make the decisions him- or herself. This usually means that there must be an assessment of whether someone can be *involved* in the decision-making process in any way.

This must be reflected in the way you use the guidelines for breaking bad news. You cannot go against the Mental Capacity Act, even if families, carers or professionals feel strongly that it would be better to protect someone from information and involvement (e.g. deciding to withhold information because it would upset the person). The purpose of the Mental Capacity Act is to allow adults to make as many decisions as they can for themselves. The legislation is supplemented by a code of practice (Department for Constitutional Affairs 2007).

What does the Mental Capacity Act say about capacity?

Every person should be presumed to be able to make their own decisions. You can only make a decision for someone else if 'all practicable steps' to help them to make a decision have been taken without success. The Mental Capacity Act is not specific about what exactly 'all practicable steps' includes, but it can be assumed that it means taking time and making information accessible, for example, through easy language or pictures.

People can have capacity to decide some things, but not others; or to decide something at some times, but not other times. For example, someone might have capacity to decide that he wants to have radiotherapy, but his needle phobia means that he does not have capacity to decide whether or not to have a blood test – his panic renders him temporarily incapacitated to take that particular decision.

Incapacity is not based on the ability to make a wise or sensible decision. People may go against the advice of their doctors, nurses and families. Furthermore, it is not based on a condition or an aspect of someone's behaviour – you cannot say that someone lacks capacity simply because he has Down's syndrome, for instance.

How 'mental incapacity' is determined

A person is unable to make a decision if he cannot:

1. understand the information relevant to the decision
2. retain that information (it is OK to retain it just long enough to make the decision)
3. use or weigh that information as part of the process of making the decision
4. communicate the decision.

Making decisions for someone: 'best interest'

If, having taken all practical steps to assist someone, it is concluded that a decision should be made for him, that decision must be made in that person's best interest. The Mental Capacity Act sets out a checklist of things to consider when deciding what is in a person's best interest. You should:

- not make assumptions on the basis of age, appearance, condition or behaviour
- consider all the relevant circumstances
- consider whether or when someone will have capacity to make the decision
- support someone's participation in any acts or decisions made for him
- not make a decision about life-sustaining treatment 'motivated by a desire to bring about his (or her) death'
- consider someone's expressed wishes and feelings, beliefs and values; these can be expressed in non-verbal ways
- consult and take into account the views of others, including those with an interest in someone's welfare – such as those engaged in caring for the person.

ASSESSING CAPACITY FOR JEREMY AND CHRISTINA

In Example A (Chapter 22), Jeremy's and Christina's capacity had to be assessed in order to make sure that the treatment decision was theirs (if they had capacity) or was based on their best interest (if they didn't). This involved giving them information about their illness and treatment options in a way they were most likely to understand.

Jeremy was given information in easy words and pictures about the treatment options and the likely consequences. This needed several sessions over a number of days. Jeremy was able to:

1. explain the options back to the nurse in his own words
2. keep the information in his head for long enough to make a decision
3. explain the pros and cons of not having the treatment (which included him answering *'I'm going to die'* when asked what the effect will be of not having the operation)
4. communicate his wishes clearly.

He therefore has capacity to make a treatment decision, and his wishes must be abided by.

Christina, on the other hand, did not have capacity. She understood that there were two treatment options (to have the operation, or not to have it); but she could not weigh up the long-term consequences of these options. The decision not to operate was a 'best interest' decision, made by the medical team in consultation with her family and care staff. They took into account Christina's clear wish to eat and her previous difficulties in coping with being in hospital.

RESOURCES

The Breaking Bad News website (**www.breakingbadnews.org**), set up by the author, contains a summary of the information described in this book, as well as some further links and resources. The author welcomes feedback and comments. Please email her at **info@ breakingbadnews.org**.

RESOURCES FOR PEOPLE WITH INTELLECTUAL DISABILITIES
Books Beyond Words
Books Beyond Words is a series of picture books that has been developed to make communicating easier for these people with intellectual disabilities, and to enable discussion about difficult topics. The pictures are designed to help the reader make sense of what is happening to them, and help them to ask questions or share their concerns. Supporting text and guidelines are also provided for carers, supporters and professionals. Published by RCPsych/St George's, University of London. Available from **www.booksbeyondwords. co.uk**. The website also includes a video and advice on how to use the books.

Selected useful titles:

Am I Going to Die? by *Sheila Hollins and Irene Tuffrey-Wijne* (2009). It tells the story of a man who has intellectual disabilities and who is terminally ill, showing how he is affected by the physical and emotional aspects of dying. It highlights the importance of making good use of the time left, and of saying goodbyes.

When Dad Died and *When Mum Died* both by Sheila Hollins and Lester Sireling (1989). These books tell the story of the death of a parent in an honest, straightforward and moving way.

When Somebody Dies by Sheila Hollins, Noëlle Blackman and Sandra Dowling (2003). The book shows how two people are upset when someone they love dies, but friends and counselling help them to deal with their grief.

Ann Has Dementia by Sheila Hollins (2012). This book shows what happens to Ann as her dementia causes her to behave in an unusual way. Her family doctor and supporter try to provide the right care for her at home in the early days of her dementia, until Ann becomes so confused that she moves into residential care.

We're Living Well but Dying Matters
A video about including people with intellectual disabilities in discussions about death, dying and bereavement. It shows a group of people with intellectual disabilities discussing what they would like to happen when they die.

Easy-read accessible books about cancer
CHANGE (www.changepeople.co.uk), the rights organization for people with learning disabilities, produce three titles, each with an illustrated book for people with intellectual disabilities and a book for carers:
- *Symptoms, Screening and Staying Healthy*
- *Diagnosis and Treatment*
- *Palliative Care, End of Life Care and Bereavement.*

BOOKS
Living with Learning Disabilities, Dying with Cancer: Thirteen Personal Stories by Irene Tuffrey-Wijne (2010). London: Jessica Kingsley Publishers.
An account of the experiences of 13 people with intellectual disabilities who were living with cancer, most of whom died. It includes a discussion of how people with intellectual disabilities

RESOURCES 179

can best be supported at the end of life. The book is the fore-runner to this work on breaking bad news.

Caring for People with Learning Disabilities Who Are Dying by *Noëlle Blackman and Stuart Todd* (2005). London: Worth Publishing.
A concise, clearly written and practical book full of advice for service managers and staff working in intellectual disability services.

Loss and Learning Disability by *Noëlle Blackman* (2003). London: Worth Publishing.
This book is for care staff, therapists and counsellors working with people with intellectual disabilities. It talks about how people with intellectual disabilities can be affected by bereavement. It includes ways to prevent normal grief from becoming a bigger problems and ways of helping people when the grief process 'goes wrong'.

USEFUL SERVICES AND ORGANIZATIONS

Community Teams for People with Intellectual Disabilities. These are specialist multidisciplinary health teams that support adults with intellectual disabilities and their families and carers by assessment, by supporting access to mainstream health care, and by providing a range of clinical interventions. Your GP or social services department should have the details of your local team.

Help the Hospices (www.helpthehospices.org.uk/hospice information; phone: 020 7520 8222). Provides information about hospice care and about locally available hospice and palliative care services.

Macmillan Information Line (www.macmillan.org.uk; phone: 0808 808 2020). Provides practical, emotional, medical and financial advice for people affected by cancer in general. Also provides information about Macmillan services as well as other cancer organizations and support agencies.

Palliative Care of People with Learning Disabilities (PCPLD) Network (www.pcpld.org; email: info@pcpld.org). Encourages and contributes to the development of good practice in the palliative care of people with intellectual disabilities, through networking and organizing national and regional study days.

Cruse Bereavement Care (www.cruse.org.uk; email: helpline@ cruse.org.uk; phone: 0844 477 9400). Offers free bereavement counselling, support and information to anyone affected by death (including paid carers).

Respond (www.respond.org.uk; phone: 0808 808 0700). This London-based charity supports people with intellectual disabilities, their carers and professionals around any issue of trauma (including bereavement) by offering advice, training and psychotherapy.

Skylight Trust (www.skylight.org.nz/Breaking+Bad+News). A New Zealand-based organization supporting people in traumatic situations. The website has very useful guidelines on supporting children and teens through bereavement.

The National Autistic Society (www.autism.org.uk; email: nas@ nas.org.uk; phone: 020 7833 2299). The services of this charity include advice, information and training on all aspects of autism.

Carers UK (www.carersuk.org; phone (London branch): 020 7378 4999). A UK charity set up to help and support people who care for family or friends.

Alzheimer's Society (http://alzheimers.org.uk; helpline: 0845 300 0336). Telephone and online services provide information on all aspects of living with dementia. As a support and research charity, this is a membership organization working to improve the quality of life of people affected by dementia in England, Wales and Northern Ireland.

Mencap (www.mencap.org.uk; email: information@mencap.org. uk; phone: 020 7454 0454). A campaigning charity in the UK working closely with people with intellectual disabilities and carers to improve lives. Also provides a wide range of information and resources on living with intellectual disabilities.

WEBSITES

www.gmc-uk.org/learningdisabilities The website of the General Medical Council has a useful section for doctors and other general health care staff on people with intellectual disabilities, addressing issues of assessment and communication. There is also a helpful Resources page.

www.intellectualdisability.info This website, hosted by St George's, University of London, is a comprehensive learning resource for medical, nursing and other health care students on understanding issues around intellectual disabilities and health. It includes guidance on communication and consent.

REFERENCES

Buckman, R. (1984) 'Breaking bad news – Why is it still so difficult?' *British Medical Journal 288*, 1597–1599.

Buckman, R. (1992) *How to Break Bad News: A Guide for Health Care Professionals.* Baltimore, MD: The Johns Hopkins University Press.

Department for Constitutional Affairs (2007) *Mental Capacity Act 2005: Code of Practice.* London: The Stationery Office.

Girgis, A. and Sanson-Fisher, R. (1995) 'Breaking bad news: Consensus guidelines for medical practitioners.' *Journal of Clinical Oncology 13*, 99, 2449–2456.

Mehrabian, A. (1981) *Silent Messages: Implicit Communication of Emotions and Attitudes* (2nd edn). Belmont, CA: Wadsworth Publishing.

Oken, D. (1961) 'What to tell cancer patients: A study of medical attitudes.' *Journal of the American Medical Association 175*, 13, 1120–1128.

The NHS Information Centre (2011) *Data on Written Complaints in the NHS 2010–11*. Workforce and Facilities Team. Leeds: The Health and Social Care Information Centre.

Tuffrey-Wijne, I. (2010) *Living with Learning Disabilities, Dying with Cancer: Thirteen Personal Stories.* London: Jessica Kingsley Publishers.

FURTHER READING

Arber, A. and Gallagher, A. (2003) 'Breaking bad news revisited: The push for negotiated disclosure and changing practice implications.' *International Journal of Palliative Nursing 9*, 4, 166–172.

Baile, W., Buckman, R., Lenzi, R., Glober, G., Beale, E. and Kudelka, A. (2005) 'SPIKES – a six-step protocol for delivering bad news: Application to the patient with cancer.' *The Oncologist 5*, 4, 302–311.

Bernal, J. and Tuffrey-Wijne, I. (2008) 'Telling the truth – or not: Disclosure and information for people with intellectual disabilities who have cancer.' *International Journal on Disability and Human Development 7*, 4, 365–370.

Blackman, N. and Todd, S. (2005) *Caring for People with Learning Disabilities Who Are Dying: A Practical Guide for Carers.* London: Worth Publishing.

Breaking Bad News. Available at www.breakingbadnews.org.

Cogher, L. (2010) 'Communication with Children and Young People.' In G. Grant, P. Ramcharan, M. Flynn and M. Richardson (eds) *Learning Disability: A Life Cycle Approach* (2nd edn). Maidenhead: Open University Press.

Department of Health (2001) *Valuing People: A New Strategy for Learning Disability for the 21st Century.* A White Paper. London: Department of Health.

Eggly, S., Penner, L. and Albrecht, T. (2006) 'Discussing bad news in the outpatient oncology clinic: Rethinking current communication guidelines.' *Journal of Clinical Oncology 24*, 4, 716–719.

Emerson, E. and Hatton, C. (2008) *People with Learning Disabilities in England.* Lancaster: Centre for Disability Research.

Fujimori, M. and Uchitomi, Y. (2009) 'Preferences of cancer patients regarding communication of bad news: A systematic literature review.' *Japanese Journal of Clinical Oncology 39*, 4, 201–216.

Iacono, T. (2004) 'Patients with disabilities and complex communication needs: The GP consultation.' *Australian Family Physician 33*, 8, 585–589.

Innes, S. and Payne, S. (2009) 'Advanced cancer patients' prognostic information preferences: A review.' *Palliative Medicine 23*, 1, 29–39.

Kaye, P. (1996) *Breaking Bad News: A 10 Step Approach.* Northampton: EPL Publications.

Knott, L. (2010) *Breaking Bad News.* Available at www.patient.co.uk/doctor/Breaking-Bad-News.htm, accessed on 29 March 2012.

McEnhill, L. (2008) 'Breaking bad news of cancer to people with learning disabilities.' *British Journal of Learning Disabilities 36*, 3, 157–164.

Novack, D., Plumer, R., Smith, R., Ochitill, H., Morrow, G. and Bennett, J. (1971) 'Changes in physicians' attitudes toward telling the cancer patient.' *Journal of the American Medical Association 241*, 9, 897–900.

Read, S. (1998) 'Breaking bad news to people who have a learning disability.' *British Journal of Nursing 7*, 2, 86–91.

Schalock, R., Borthwick-Duffy, S., Bradley, V. *et al.* (2010) *Intellectual Disability: Definition, Classification, and System of Supports* (11th edn). Washington, DC: AAIDD.

Seale, C. (1991) 'Communication and awareness about death: A study of a random sample of dying people.' *Social Sciences and Medicine 32*, 8, 943–952.

Skylight Trust (2007) 'Breaking bad news to children and teens.' Information sheet. Newtown: Skylight Trust. Available at www.skylight.org.nz/uploads/files/breaking_bad_news_to_children_and_teens.pdf, accessed on 29 March 2012.

The National Autistic Society. Available at www.autism.org.uk.

Tuffrey-Wijne, I. (2012) 'A new model for breaking bad news to people with intellectual disabilities.' *Palliative Medicine*, doi:10.1177/0269216311433476.

Tuffrey-Wijne, I., Bernal, J. and Hollins, S. (2010) 'Disclosure and understanding of cancer diagnosis and prognosis for people with intellectual disabilities: Findings from an ethnographic study.' *European Journal of Oncology Nursing 14*, 3, 224–230.

World Health Organization (1992) *ICD-10: The Tenth Revision of the International Statistical Classification of Diseases and Related Health Problems.* Geneva: World Health Organization.

INDEX